Priests and Cobblers

Leonard Broom, *General Editor*
L. L. Langness, *Editor*

STUDIES IN SOCIAL AND ECONOMIC CHANGE
Philip H. Gulliver and David J. Parkin, *Editors*

Priests and Cobblers

A Study of Social Change in a Hindu Village in Western Nepal

A. PATRICIA CAPLAN

CHANDLER PUBLISHING COMPANY
An Intext Publisher
SAN FRANCISCO • SCRANTON • LONDON • TORONTO

Library of Congress Cataloging in Publication Data

Caplan, A   Patricia.
    Priests and cobblers.

    (Studies in social and economic change)
    Bibliography: p.
    1. Villages—Nepal.   2. Nepal—Social conditions.   3. Nepal—Economic conditions.
    I. Title.
HN761.N42C35   301.3'52'095496   77–179033
ISBN 0–8102–0454–1

COPYRIGHT © 1972 BY CHANDLER PUBLISHING COMPANY
ALL RIGHTS RESERVED
INTERNATIONAL STANDARD BOOK NUMBER 0–8102–0454–1
LIBRARY OF CONGRESS CATALOG CARD NUMBER 77–179033
PRINTED IN THE UNITED STATES OF AMERICA

For my parents

CONTENTS

TABLES

MAPS

FOREWORD

It is the intention of this series to present monographs each of which deals with a particular group of people, without seeking to define that phrase too narrowly. Monographs focus on, for example, an African ethnic group, a South Asian caste village or group of villages, and the people of a Pacific island. Each monograph is self-sufficient in its own right and not directly dependent on others in the series, and each is written by an anthropologist who has recently carried out field research in the area concerned.

The focus of each study is on economic, political, and cultural changes, their causes, processes, and consequences during the twentieth century among the selected group of people, and with particular reference to the preceding two decades or so. The primary aim is to describe the changes that have occurred and to give an explanation of the processes involved and their implications. Although broader generalizations (including comparative references to cases and processes elsewhere) are not neglected, it is not a major concern of the series to seek to establish or promote a particular theoretical approach or conclusion. Each author is asked to go beyond description and to make an analysis involving theoretical considerations according to his own preferences.

In the preparation of this series we recognized the necessary diversities of research interests and opportunities, and of theoretical orientation, but nevertheless asked each author, as far as possible, to include the following:

a. in relatively brief outline, the description of a fairly clear and relevant socioeconomic baseline from which to present the account of change (for example, immediately prior to the establishment of colonial rule, or of the achievement of independence, or of the introduction of some major, radical innovation of a technological or social nature);

b. an account of the factors responsible for producing and developing changes and of the agencies through which those factors operated; the initial reactions of the people to these factors and agencies, including the perceptions of the people about them;

c. a description and analysis of the various changes, taking account both of time sequences and of different aspects or parts of the society and culture; the identification of key roles such as those of innovator, entrepreneur, and reactionary (we asked for description to be reinforced, if possible, with quantitative data on such matters as crop production, school attendance, religious converts, and voting in elections);

d. a consideration of sequences of changes within a single field of activity (such as agriculture) and the extent to which there were concomitant changes in other fields of activity (for example, the association of agricultural change with modes of economic cooperation, family organization, religious beliefs and practices, and political action);

e. a summing up of the processes of change in the context of anthropological theory.

We encourage each author to make a serious attempt to cover a wide range of social and cultural changes among the selected people, but acknowledge his legitimate preference to emphasize certain processes of change on which he has most data and theoretical interest.

P. H. GULLIVER
D. J. PARKIN

ACKNOWLEDGEMENTS

The field-work on which this book is based was conducted from January to December 1969, as part of a project of research on aspects of social change in Nepal, sponsored by the Social Science Research Council of Great Britain. Funds for the project were administered by the School of Oriental and African Studies. I offer my thanks to these institutions for their generous assistance.

I am grateful to His Majesty's Government of Nepal for permission to conduct research there, and to those officials both in Kathmandu, and in the area of field-work, who were unfailingly courteous and helpful. Thanks are also due to Tribhuvan University for interest shown in the project.

Periods spent in Kathmandu for purposes of preparation, organization of field notes, and recuperation were made pleasant by the facilities offered by the Nepal Research Center, and I take this opportunity of thanking its director Professor Dr. W. Hellmich of Munich University. I must also record my gratitude to Mr. G. B. Kalikote, warden of the Center in Kathmandu, who helped in innumerable practical ways.

In the field I was assisted by Mr. Hari Bahadur Koirala, Mr. Khagendra Bahadur Malla, and Mr. Arun Kiran Pradhan, to all of whom thanks are due. Most of all, I express my appreciation to the people of the village in which I worked, here called Duari, for the patience with which they responded to my endless questions.

Others have contributed to the writing of this book. Firstly, I must mention Professor C. von Fürer-Haimendorf, director of the Nepal project, who encouraged my interest in the Himalayas, and made my field-work possible by the offer of a research assistantship. He has also read the final draft and made valuable suggestions. The editors of this series, Professor P. H. Gulliver and Dr. D. J. Parkin, read the manuscript with care and offered helpful comments, as did Professor A. C. Mayer. Finally, I must thank my husband, Dr. L. Caplan, not only for reading drafts of this work at various stages of its development, but also for giving much-needed encouragement.

Priests and Cobblers

1. Introduction

The Problem

This is a study of the changes which have come about in the past two decades in relations between high castes (particularly Priests or Brahmins) and untouchables (most of them Cobblers) in a Hindu village in the hills of western Nepal. Particular attention is paid to shifts in the economic and political links between the two groups since 1951, when Nepal emerged from a century of isolation from the outside world and internal stagnation under a despotic regime. Since then, the country has been opened up by new methods of communication, such as roads, airfields, and radio telegraph; educational facilities have been established; a new system of *panchayats* based on elected councils has replaced the traditional autocracy; a new constitution and a legal code, giving equal rights to all citizens, have been promulgated; land reform has attempted to redress some of the economic inequalities which have persisted for so long. This study examines the effects of these and other recent national innovations on a village community.

However, the static and unchanging nature of western Nepalese society before 1951 must not be overemphasized. It will become evident that change was already taking place at local levels prior to that date, mainly because of increasing pressure of population on land, which appears to have reached its crisis point in the first three decades of this century. Change was also the result of a chronic shortage of cash, needed for paying taxes and purchasing certain essential commodities which had to be imported. Those in a position to obtain cash—particularly the Brahmins, who received it from their clients—were able to become extremely wealthy and powerful. They lent money to members of other castes and took land on mortgage in return; they also bought land in the village. Much of the land which was sold and mortgaged belonged to untouchables, who had only limited access to cash. The latter became progressively poorer and more dependent upon the Brahmins for the wherewithal to make ends meet. The only way out of the vicious circle of indebtedness and landlessness was for untouchables to migrate to India for varying periods in search of unskilled work.

Since 1951, the district capital, very near the village, has expanded, and opportunities to earn cash locally have grown apace. The flow of cash into the district and the village has increased enormously. At the same time, the poorer sections of the village population have benefited from the opening up of a new rice-growing area a short distance south of the district, where grain is obtainable at half the local prices. Many untouchables and members of other castes now depend on obtaining their grain cheaply from this area.

A period in which the untouchables became increasingly dependent upon the Brahmins for cash and grain has therefore been followed by one of new economic opportunities for all castes, and, although the untouchables have not succeeded in raising their overall economic status, they have become increasingly independent of the Brahmins.

This has had important political repercussions. The establishment of an elected council led to bitter factional fighting in the village. At first, the factions followed the lines of an existing cleavage, based largely on high-caste clan affiliation. But soon the leaders of high-caste factions realised the electoral importance of the untouchables, who number half the village population. In recent years, the composition of factions has changed: one faction consists mostly of high-castes, and the other has a largely untouchable membership. It would be an oversimplification to describe this process purely as a change from conflict on "vertical" to conflict on "horizontal" lines, although this is certainly the idiom in which it is phrased in the village. However, there is little doubt that the untouchables would be unable to act against the high castes, had they not achieved a large measure of economic independence.

An important argument which underlies my analysis is that change is not uni-causal; there is no single, independent variable. In order to reach a full understanding of recent events in the village which I call Duari[1], the relationship between a number of variables—what Beals (1955) terms "interplay among factors of change"—must be examined.

The Setting: Belaspur District

Belaspur District, in which Duari, the focal village of this study is located, lies 250 miles from Nepal's capital, Kathmandu, and forms part of the Far Western Hills of the kingdom. This hill range lies between the high Himalayas on Nepal's northern frontier, and the low-level *terai* (a belt of marshy, jungle land) to the south, which borders the north Indian Gangetic plain. The altitude in Belaspur District varies between 2,500 and 10,000 feet, but Duari village, which lies two miles from Belaspur Bazaar, capital of the district, is at an altitude of 4,500 feet. The climate is thus not extreme, the daytime temperatures varying from 60° F. in the winter to around 90° F. in the summer. Most of the annual precipitation of 45 inches occurs during the monsoon months from June to September, but the rainfall in this area is the lowest in Nepal; the eastern part of the country, for example, receives around 75 inches of rain annually.

Partly because of the low rainfall, the Far Western Hills have the highest *per capita* deficit in cereal grain production; they also have the lowest amount of arable land *per capita* of any area in the kingdom, even though the density of the population is the lowest in the country. According to one government estimate,[2] only 23 percent of the arable land is irrigated, and for various reasons, such as steep slopes and poor drainage, vast areas cannot be cultivated. The major crops

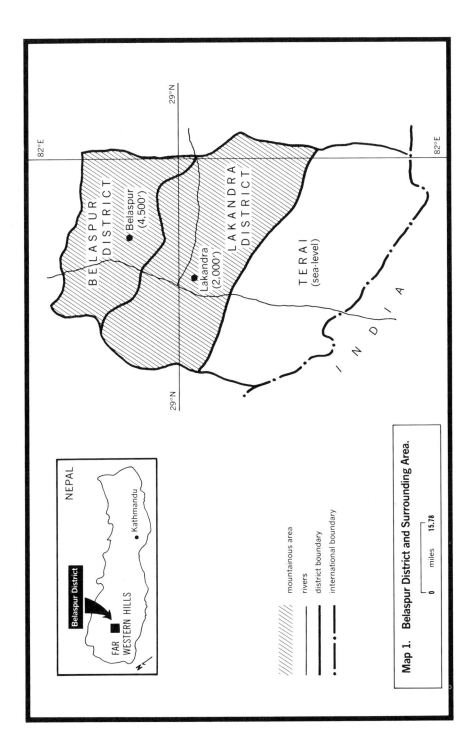

Map 1. Belaspur District and Surrounding Area.

NEPAL

Belaspur District

FAR WESTERN HILLS

• Kathmandu

BELASPUR DISTRICT

• Belaspur
(4,500')

LAKANDRA DISTRICT

Lakandra
(2,000')

TERAI
(sea-level)

I N D I A

82°E

82°E

29°N

29°N

mountainous area

rivers

district boundary

international boundary

0 ⊢ miles ⊣ 15.78

3

of rice, maize, and wheat are grown on steep, terraced slopes, laboriously carved out of the hillsides.

The Far Western Hills are considered to be the least developed part of Nepal. No motorable roads exist, and there are only a few dry-weather airfields, which have been established during the past decade, including one in a valley to the south, two days' walk from Belaspur. Until the recent introduction of radio telegraph in some of the district capitals, communication with Kathmandu was through messengers travelling on foot. There are no industries in the area, and all manufactured goods, as well as some of the grain needed to make up for local deficits, are carried in by porters from the valley to the south and from the terai, which represents a journey of about a week. The great majority of the population is dependent upon the land for its living, although in and around the district capital government service has become increasingly important, and so has trade.

Population

Belaspur District, covering an area of about 800 square miles, has a population of approximately 137,000 persons, divided into a number of castes, whose distribution is shown in Table 1.

TABLE 1. THE POPULATION OF BELASPUR DISTRICT (by Caste)

caste name	percentage of population
high castes	
Chetri	32.8
Thakuri	13.0
Jaisi	10.6
Jogi	1.9
Brahmin	1.7
other clean castes	
Magar	11.9
Gurung	0.8
Newar	0.4
Other	0.1
TOTAL CLEAN-CASTE POPULATION	73.0
Untouchables	
Metalworker (Smith)	18.8
Tailor	5.0
Cobbler	2.8
Other	0.4
TOTAL UNTOUCHABLE POPULATION	27.0

NOTE. These percentages are derived from the voting lists collected in 1969 by the district council and therefore represent only a rough approximation of the total population. Lists were available from 56 of the 57 Administrative Villages in the district. Had figures for the missing unit been available, the proportion of Brahmins in the whole district might well have been slightly higher, as it contains a rather large concentration of members of that caste.

At the top of the caste hierarchy in this area[3] are the Brahmins, who serve the other clean castes as priests. Next to them are the Jaisis, said to be the descendants of Brahmin men who married Brahmin widows. Jaisis cannot serve as priests, but they often practice as astrologers.

Thakuris and Chetris are both classed as Kshatriyas, the Hindu warrior *varna* (caste category), but the Thakuris are accorded higher status, mainly because they are thought to be the descendants of Rajputs who, like the Brahmins, fled India at the time of the Moghul invasions, and because they have traditionally provided most of the ruling families of Nepal. The Shah dynasty, which has provided the kings of Nepal for the past two hundred years, is Thakuri, and so were most of the chiefs of the petty kingdoms which flourished in various parts of western Nepal, including Belaspur District, up to as recently as 1960.

Brahmins, Jaisis, Thakuris, and Chetris are regarded as "twice-born", and their men wear the sacred thread of the high Hindu castes. The only other group in the area included in this category is the Jogis, who are regarded as a caste. They are descendants of high-caste men and women who became ascetics but were unable to keep their vows of celibacy. Jogis are known by various names, such as Puri, Giri, Sanyasi, and so forth. In Belaspur most Jogis call themselves Giri.

The clean castes in this area may be divided into two main categories on the basis of race, language, and culture. Those already discussed are of Aryan stock and speak Nepali (a Sanskrit-derived language) as their mother tongue. For convenience, they, together with the untouchables described below, are referred to as Hindus, to distinguish them from the Mongoloid peoples, who speak Tibeto-Burman languages, and who may be referred to as tribals. In fact, although tribal peoples like Magars and Gurungs have in this area retained something of a separate culture, they have become increasingly "Hinduized" and mostly speak Nepali. They are treated as ritually clean by the high castes (water is accepted from them, and they have the services of Brahmin priests), but they do not wear the sacred thread and rank below the castes already described. They also differ from the high castes in that they consume alcohol and keep pigs and chickens. For this reason they are referred to as *matwali,* or drinking castes. With the exception of the Brahmins from whose ranks the priests are drawn, no clean caste is associated with a specific traditional occupation; all are agriculturalists.

The Newars, a third category, who number only a few in this area, nearly all live in the district capital, where they form the largest single group. They are the descendants of immigrants from Kathmandu Valley. Newars are internally divided into a number of sub-castes, both Hindu and Buddhist,[4] although only a few of these are represented in Belaspur. The majority of Newars here are clean-caste Hindus, although they do not wear the sacred thread; they are mainly engaged in shopkeeping. There is also a sizeable minority of untouchable Newar Butchers (Kasai).

The remainder of the population of Belaspur District is composed of untouchables, or ritually unclean castes. They have low status because of their association with polluting activities, such as skinning dead cattle. This means that none of the clean castes will take food or water from them and will avoid physical contact where possible. Although untouchables consider themselves Hindus, they are not served by Brahmin priests and, indeed, are considered as being outside the formal Hindu hierarchy by members of clean castes. Untouchables are, however, necessary to the proper functioning of the caste system, since they provide services which clean-caste persons are precluded from performing. Not all the untouchables in this area perform their traditional occupations; indeed, the majority earn a living through farming their own lands and working for others as unskilled labourers. Those who still do work as functionaries are often bound to clean-caste families in a more-or-less permanent *jajmani*-type relationship.[5] On the whole, untouchables form the lowest economic, as well as social and ritual, stratum of the society.

History

From the eleventh to the fourteenth centuries, what are now the Far Western Hills of Nepal were a part of the Malla kingdom, whose jurisdiction extended as far as western Tibet.[6] Stone pillars and temples dating from this period, some with inscriptions in Sanskrit and Tibetan, abound in the region. With the collapse of the Malla dynasty, the kingdom broke up and, by the fourteenth century, had been replaced by about fifty small principalities under Thakuri rulers, who had fled India along with many other Hindus during the Moghul invasions of the previous centuries. The area surrounding Duari village became part of the principality of Belaspur, ruled by a king *(rajah)* from a palace said to have been located just east of the village.[7] This kingship, along with most of the others, disappeared when the rulers of Gorkha, a small kingdom east of Belaspur, conquered most of the Himalayan region between Sikkim and Kumaon, including the Kathmandu Valley, during the latter half of the eighteenth century and thus founded the modern state of Nepal.[8] The country has been ruled by the Shah royal family, descendants of the Gorkha chief who led the conquering armies, since that date. In 1846, however, the Ranas, an influential Chetri family in Kathmandu, succeeded in gaining complete control of the government, and for the next hundred years the Shah kings were secluded puppets while the autocratic Ranas ruled the country.

Under the Rana regime the country was divided into thirty-five districts, of which Belaspur was one. Each district was under the control of a governor *(bada hakim)*, who, although responsible to the government in Kathmandu, exercised considerable power because of the lack of communication with the capital. The governor was commander of the local militia and, at one time, had overall responsibility for various branches of the administration in the district: the court, the treasury office, and the postal services. The governor was invariably an outsider appointed from Kathmandu, as were most of his senior officials. But the majority of junior civil servants, such as clerks, messengers, grooms, and soldiers, were recruited from the local population.

The lowest levels of local government were revenue units, whose jurisdiction frequently coincided with villages, each under the control of a headman *(mukhiya)* who was responsible for collecting taxes from the inhabitants. Revenue units in a district sub-division were grouped under a senior headman *(jimmawal),* who collected the taxes from the headmen in his assigned area and, after deducting a small percentage, paid them to the treasury office in the district capital.

In 1951 the Rana regime was overthrown and power fully restored to the royal family. For a time, there was uncertainty and confusion at both national and local levels. Political parties were legalised for the first time, but parliamentary elections were not held until 1959. They were won by the Nepali Congress Party, the party which had been instrumental in overthrowing the Ranas. However, representative democracy in Nepal was short-lived: in 1960 the king dissolved the parliament, and outlawed political parties. They were replaced by a system of elected village, district, and national councils (panchayat).

The new panchayat system was accompanied by a change in the administrative structure. Nepal was divided into fourteen "development zones" and seventy-five "development districts". Belaspur District was halved in size, and the southern portion was made a separate district. Belaspur, together with this and three other contiguous districts, now forms one zone. Zonal headquarters are in the terai.

Villages were also reorganised. The new Administrative Villages were generally larger units than those previously controlled by headmen, and frequently, as happened with Duari, several revenue units/villages were amalgamated to form one. In order to avoid confusion, I shall use the word *village* to refer to settlements such as Duari, which are distinguished by name and geography from like settlements, and *Administrative Village* to refer to the new units.

Each Administrative Village is divided into nine wards, and the inhabitants of each ward elect one representative to the village council. The chairman *(pradhan panch)* and vice-chairman of the council are elected by universal adult suffrage. The council then elects one of its number to serve on the district assembly, from whose ranks the members of the district council are elected. Members of the district council then participate in a zonal assembly, which chooses the district representative to the national assembly in Kathmandu. Thus, it is only at the lowest level that people have a direct say in government.

Belaspur Bazaar

This small town has existed since at least the end of the eighteenth century, when the victorious Gorkhas built a stone fort there, still used by the militia. Until the 1951 revolution, however, there were only a handful of offices and shops, a few temples, and, later on, a religious school. The growth of the bazaar since that date has been dramatic, with the establishment of nine new government and quasi-governmental offices and the district's first and only high school. There has also been a great increase in the number of shops, from perhaps a dozen before the revolution to around seventy in 1969. The shops are mostly small and carry a limited range of goods, such as cloth, trinkets, cigarettes, tea, sugar, and kerosene, all imported from India via the terai. Prices of manufactured goods are extremely high in Belaspur, particularly during the hot season (April through June) when porters' wages rise considerably. During the monsoon which follows, the flow of goods tends to stop altogether, as Belaspur is often cut off from the south by swollen rivers.

Duari Village

Duari village, two miles north of the bazaar, sprawls over a hillside, with its widely scattered houses connected by steep and winding paths. It covers about fifteen square miles, but most of the settlement is in the dry fields used for growing wheat and maize, which lie on the upper slopes; below these are the irrigated rice fields which drop down to the river, some 2,000 feet below the crest of the ridge.

Houses in Duari vary considerably in size and quality. Some are slate-tiled and have several storeys and many rooms; such houses may also have separate out-buildings for animals. These are the houses of richer, high-caste families. Poorer people have thatched houses of two rooms, built one on top of the other. The upper room is used for sleeping, cooking, and eating, and the lower room houses the animals. All houses are built of a wooden framework, which is filled in with stones held together by mud. The walls are plastered smooth and usually white-washed. The doorways are low, and windows and chimneys non-existent, so that the interiors tend to be dark and smoky. At the front of each house is a little courtyard, where grain is dried and pounded, adults sit and talk, and children play.

In this part of Nepal, village boundaries are clearly demarcated, even though there may not be any obvious geographical division. To the north of Duari lies a small village, Magargaon, and to the north-east, an even smaller Hindu village, Toli; both are now incorporated with Duari in a single Administrative Village. Natural boundaries are provided to the east by the crest of the ridge and the main, northward trail, and to the west by the river valley (see Map 2). The only other village contiguous with Duari lies to the south-west; this is inhabited mainly by Chetris, one of whom was formerly the senior headman of the area. On the lower slopes of the ridge and to the north and south of the village lie areas of forest, used for grazing cattle and collecting firewood. However, much of the forest has been lost to the demands for arable land, and what remains is protected by government legislation. Aside from the forest, there is almost no virgin land available for cultivation in the vicinity of the village. The little which is still unused is mostly on slopes too steep for the construction of terraces, or remains untouched because it is too stony to support plant growth.

Although Duari is clearly recognised by its inhabitants as a unit, it has few communal facilities or meeting places. There are no shops in the village, nor is there a village shrine or temple; the villagers worship a number of different gods

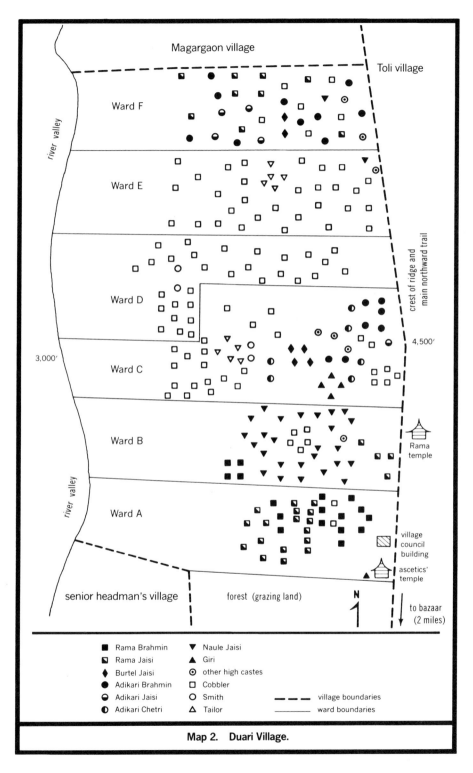

Map 2. Duari Village.

Magargaon village

Toli village

river valley

Ward F

Ward E

crest of ridge and
main northward trail

Ward D

4,500'

3,000'

Ward C

Ward B

Rama
temple

river valley

Ward A

village
council
building

ascetics'
temple

senior headman's village

forest (grazing land)

N

to bazaar
(2 miles)

■ Rama Brahmin ▼ Naule Jaisi
◪ Rama Jaisi ▲ Giri
◆ Burtel Jaisi ⊙ other high castes
● Adikari Brahmin □ Cobbler
◒ Adikari Jaisi ○ Smith   ─ ─ ─ village boundaries
◑ Adikari Chetri △ Tailor   ───── ward boundaries

The houses of upper Duari village lie scattered over a hillside among terraced fields of ripe maize.

whose temples mostly lie outside the confines of the village. Duari has no school of its own; some children go to school in Belaspur Bazaar, and others in the northern part of the village find it more convenient to attend the school in Magargaon (which is officially designated as the Administrative Village school). In the past few years, a village council building has been constructed at the instigation of the government, but this is only used on the occasion of village assemblies or council meetings.

Villagers tended formerly to gather at the houses of rich and influential men, particularly the headman, whose revenue unit was coterminous with the village. Later, with the abolition of the traditional system of tax collection and the replacement of the headman by a village council chairman, the latter's house became the gathering place. However, more recently, village men have begun to meet one another in Belaspur Bazaar, particularly in the shops owned by influential fellow-villagers. This is partly because the present chairman lives in the northernmost ward of the village, which is isolated from the main settlement area (see Map 2) and also because of the greater number of ties villagers now have with the bazaar.

Population: Caste and Clan

In the Administrative Village of which Duari is now a part, there are 374 households; 248 of these are in Duari itself and include a population of 1,228 persons. The breakdown of the population of Duari by caste is indicated in Table 2.

TABLE 2. THE POPULATION OF DUARI VILLAGE (by Caste).

caste	number of members	percentage of population
Jaisi	371	30.2
Brahmin	181	14.7
Chetri	43	3.5
Giri	28	2.2
Ascetic	3	0.2
Thakuri	2	0.1
TOTAL HIGH-CASTE	628	50.9
Cobbler	529	43.1
Tailor	50	4.1
Smith	21	1.7
TOTAL UNTOUCHABLE	600	48.9
TOTAL POPULATION	1,228	99.8

Duari village may thus not be taken as typical of the population of the district or, indeed, of most villages in Nepal, since it contains such a high proportion of Brahmins and Cobblers, and so few Chetris or Thakuris (see Table 1.)It is also unusual in that the population is almost evenly divided between high-castes and untouchables; in most other villages, the latter are heavily outnumbered. There is a wide status and cultural gulf between high-castes and untouchables. The latter worship at separate temples, and, although they may bring offerings to other gods worshipped by the high-castes, they may not approach the temples. Untouchables may not use the wells in the village, although they have access to the springs. They may not enter the houses of the high-castes; indeed, they may not even sit at the doorway. If an untouchable does a day's work for a high-caste household and is given a meal, he either has to use his own utensils, or else is given a leaf plate which he then throws away.

Although untouchables may buy tea like anyone else, they must sit outside tea-shops and wash the cups out themselves afterward; the shopkeeper washes the cups of high-caste customers. When speaking to an untouchable, a high-caste man uses a form of address normally reserved for status inferiors, whereas an untouchable must use a respectful form of address to a person of higher caste.

There are considerable differences in the institutions of kinship and marriage between high-castes and untouchables. The former are divided into named, patrilineal, exogamous clans, which in Duari have separate residential areas; clans are also distinguished by their worship of different gods *(kul deota)*. Untouchables also have clans, but these are not important. They are not exogamous units, nor are they associated with particular gods. Of greater importance for the untouchables are shallow lineages, within which marriages may not take place.

Because there is such a large number of Cobblers in the village, there is a very high intramarriage rate; high-castes, on the other hand, tend to marry into neighbouring villages within a day's walk of Duari. The Cobblers, then, are bound together in a web of kinship and affiinity, and they often point out that "we are all related to one another".

Untouchable boys and girls marry later than do high-castes, at about seventeen or eighteen, and they often choose their own spouses; they are certainly unlikely to marry people they do not know, which happens frequently with high-caste children. The marriages of the latter are generally arranged by the parents, often through a third party, and boys and girls are married young; girls are often married by the time they are ten, although they continue to live with their parents until they reach puberty. Brideprice is given by untouchables in the form of pigs and liquor, but no brideprice is given for a high-caste girl, although a gift of cash may be made to her parents by the family of the groom to help cover some of their expenses. Girls of all castes receive dowries from their parents and gifts of gold ornaments from their husbands.

The Cobblers have most of their important social links within the village. For the high castes this is not entirely so. Brahmins, for instance, are priests with clients over a very wide area of Belaspur District. The wealthier among them are money-lenders, with borrowers in neighbouring villages. And, as already pointed out, most marriages also take place outside the village. So the multiplex links of the high castes extend beyond the village.

Certain important ties between high-castes and untouchables will be discussed in greater detail in the following chapters; it should be noted at this point, however, that there are fewer ritual ties between them than might be found in Indian villages. The most important relationships are a form of jajmani tie, linking members of high castes to Tailors and Smiths, or plough service and agricultural labour, which links them to Cobblers. However, in addition to providing economic services, the Cobblers are charged with removing the carcasses of dead animals. They sell the skins to Cobblers in the bazaar who do the curing and make shoes. Tailors also function as Musicians and are called upon to perform at high-caste weddings and funerals and on public occasions, such as national holidays and election victory celebrations. However, many services which would be provided by occupational castes in India, such as laundering and hair cutting, the high-castes do for themselves in this part of Nepal.

Legends of Origin and Structural Divisions

Legends of origin are used by the villagers to explain present-day cleavages. These point to a fairly clear order of immigration into the village by the castes and clans now resident there. The earliest inhabitants are reported to have been Cobblers, who now live in Wards D and E (see Map 2). Their rights to cultivate land are said to have been recognised by the Belaspur king, and the following legend is recounted by the Cobblers to validate their claims:

Legend A. The Cobbler and the King

A Cobbler was the close friend of the Belaspur king, and spent much of his time at the palace, which lay just above the village.[9] There was a war between the [Hindu] king of Belaspur and a Buddhist king whose territory lay to the north. The Belaspur king defeated the Buddhist king and killed him. But one of the followers of the slain king succeeded in obtaining a post as herd-boy in the Belaspur king's palace and then stabbed him as he was bathing. The Belaspur king, realising that he was dying, called for his Cobbler friend.

When the Cobbler heard the news, he was afraid to go to the palace, for he thought he might be blamed. So he refused. Finally, the king sent messengers with orders to bring the Cobbler by force, if necessary; this time the Cobbler came. He saw that the king was dying and began to weep, and the king, who had begun to upbraid the Cobbler for deserting him in his hour of need, saw that he was genuinely sad. So he asked the Cobbler to make a request of him. The Cobbler said that he had never wanted anything and did not want anything now. The king offered him gold and jewels, but he refused. Finally, to show that he wanted nothing and that his had been a disinterested friendship, he picked up a handful of earth, and said he would take that. But the king misunderstood, and told him to take the earth and sprinkle it over as wide an area as he could traverse. When the Cobbler came back, the king told him that he and his descendants were to be tax-collectors for the whole area he had just covered. Then the king died.

It is interesting to note that this story is known not only to the Cobblers, but to most of the villagers of all castes. Indeed, it is generally agreed that the Cobblers were the earliest settlers in the village and at one time owned all the land.

It is also widely agreed that the next arrivals were two Brahmin clans, the Adikaris and the Burtels. The Cobblers assert that they "showed" these people land which they could cultivate and that relations between them were entirely amicable. The Burtels were the priests of the Adikaris, but the latter, a more numerous clan, became priests for the whole area around Duari village. They were given written authority *(lalmohor)* by one of the Belaspur kings, so they claim, to monopolise the priestly services in the area . Both Adikaris and Burtels settled in what is now Ward C of the village and soon afterward were joined by a family of Giris, descendants of ascetics.[10]

Adikaris, Burtels, and Giris had, and to some extent still maintain, a special relationship. They regard one another as agnatic kinsmen and exchange ritual marks *(tika)* at certain festivals. In theory they should not intermarry, although this rule has been broken once, when one of the Adikari Brahmins took a Giri woman; their descendants, although still Adikaris by clan, are ranked as Chetris by caste.[11] The majority of Adikaris are still Brahmins, but Burtels have lost their Brahmin status by marrying Jaisi women. Their descendants are now all Jaisis and therefore cannot function as priests. In spite of the loss of their priestly status, the Burtels are still treated with the respect due to priests by their clients, and the Adikaris take them small presents from time to time, but of course must now have their rituals performed by Brahmins of other clans.

The Adikaris, Burtels, and Giris are also bound together by their worship of Mahabe (Maha Dev), a manifestation of Shiva. The following myth is told about the establishment of the worship of Mahabe in the area and the crucial part the Adikaris played in it:

Legend B. How the Worship of Mahabe was Established

Previously, there was no Mahabe god in Belaspur. On the ridge which is now called Mahabe, the Adikaris, Burtels, and Giris used to herd their cattle together. One of the Adikaris was dumb and good-natured, and he was always left in charge of the cattle while the other youths used to go off and flirt with the girls in the forest. The Adikari man was not only dumb—he was also very simple. There were three stones on the top of the ridge, and every day when he had milked the cows, he used to pour some of the milk on the stones, thinking that in this way he would make them soft; then he would go to sleep, using the stones as pillows.

One day when he was sleeping, one of the stones rose up and broke into pieces, and the god Shiva appeared. The dumb man became able to speak immediately, and he talked with the god who had come to him because he was simple and good. But he was told to keep these miraculous happenings a secret. However, when his friends returned, they found that not only could he speak, but he even knew Sanskrit. They forced him to tell them how it had happened, but then he became dumb again and died. His companions built a temple on that spot, but it was destroyed by the god. Now there are only the two broken pieces of stone, with a *shiva-ling* [phallic symbol] between them, and the footprints of the god, made when he appeared to the dumb man in human form.

This became a sacred place for these three clans, like a temple; the Adikaris were the votaries and also used to have the rights to the land *(guthi)* attached to the place.[12] Although the Adikaris have now lost the guthi, they still lead the worship of Mahabe once a year at this spot, when Burtels and Giris also bring offerings, and they are respected as the "discoverers" of Mahabe.

It is also significant that the descendants of the Cobblers who first settled in Duari worship Mahabe, as well, although they do not go to the sacred place or to any of the Mahabe temples, and they have a separate household god (kul deota). However, they do make offerings to Mahabe, who is conceived to be the guardian of all Duari village, with the exception of Ward A, whose inhabitants worship another god.

The next immigrants into the village were said to have been members of the Naule clan, composed entirely of Jaisis. They came with a small group of Cobblers from a village south of Belaspur Bazaar and settled in Ward B. The Naules took Adikari priests.

The Tailors and the Smiths are less clear about when or whence they came to the village. The Cobblers assert that they gave land to these other untouchable groups, and, in fact, they are settled in areas of the village densely populated by Cobblers. Although there is no strict order of caste-ranking among the three groups of untouchables (they refuse commensal relations with one another) there is no intermarriage among them.

The latest immigrants, who are now the largest high-caste clan, were the Ramas, some of whom were Brahmins and some Jaisis (a few are now Chetris, descendants of unions between Jaisis and Giris). The Ramas settled in the south of the village, displacing some of the untouchables. The Brahmins among them became priests to families living in the area to the south and west of the village, thus ending the Adikari monopoly. The Ramas recount the following myth concerning their settlement in Duari:

Four ascetic Giri women pose at the door of their temple in Duari.

Legend C.   How the Ramas Won the King's Favour

The palace of the king of Belaspur was continuously being struck by lightning, and he asked for anyone who knew how to prevent this to come forward. A Rama Jaisi, who was an astrologer and a very clever man, went to the palace and fashioned a goat out of metal. This he placed on the roof of the palace, and the lightning no longer struck there. Instead, it fell upon a spot in the bazaar. The king was so delighted that he favoured the Rama clan. He built a temple to Bhairab [another manifestation of Shiva] on the spot where the lightning now fell and made the Ramas the custodians of it. He recognised their right to settle in the village. Later, when the Belaspur kingship ended, another Bhairab temple was erected on the site of the old palace, and of this temple, too, the Ramas became custodians.

The Ramas thus claim that their rights are derived directly from the Belaspur king, just as the Cobblers do. It is probably because the Ramas were the custodians of the bazaar temple that as the bazaar grew they also became the priests for the government servants, shopkeepers, and soldiers who lived there.

The distribution of groups in the village reflects most of the important divisions within village society. As can be seen from Map 2, most of the untouchables occupy a separate area in the northern part of the village (Ward D and E); a sprinkling of them is to be found in Wards B and C, where high-caste people live, too. There is also a spatial separation which corresponds to clan divisions among the high castes: the Ramas occupy Ward A, the Naules Ward B, and the Adikaris, Burtels, and Giris Ward C. The population of the high-caste clans is shown in Table 3.

TABLE 3. THE HIGH-CASTE POPULATION OF DUARI (by Clan and Caste).

clan caste	number of members[1]	percentage of high-caste population
Rama Jaisis	175	27.8
Rama Brahmins	86	13.7
Rama Chetris	11	1.7
Rama Thakuris[2]	2	0.4
RAMAS (TOTAL)	274	43.6
Adikari Brahmins	95	15.1
Adikari Jaisis	28	4.4
Adikari Chetris	21	3.4
ADIKARIS TOTAL	144	22.9
Naule Jaisis	119	18.9
Giris	28	4.4
Burtel Jaisis	25	3.9
Das Chetris[3]	10	1.6
Ascetics[4]	3	0.5
Other[5]	25	3.9
HIGH-CASTE POPULATION	628	99.7

1. Defined as male adults, their sons, their wives (a woman takes her husband's clan name on marriage), and their unmarried or divorced daughters.

2. The Rama Thakuris consist of a Thakuri woman from another village married to a Rama Brahmin. Their son is classed as a Thakuri.

3. Das Chetris are ex-slaves, who apparently belonged to the Burtels. They now wear the sacred thread and are beginning to marry other Chetris.

4. Four ascetic women tend a temple in Ward A. They have all come from outside Duari, but they now have a house next to the temple.

5. The handful of members of high-caste clans living in Wards E and F on the border with Toli, where most of their fellow-clansmen live. They interact mainly with the inhabitants of Toli; indeed, their lands and houses may at one time have fallen within the borders of that village.

Conclusion

Spatial divisions between groups and the population breakdown by caste and clan have been stressed because there are contexts in which the cleavage between the castes is relevant, whereas in others the dominant cleavage is between the clans of the high castes. The next step in the analysis is to consider economic life in the village.

NOTES

1. In accordance with a promise made to the villagers among whom I worked, all place names and proper names in this book have been changed—that is, the names of the district and village, and the first and clan names of people.

2. Nepal Government *Sample Census of Agriculture,* 1962.

3. For a discussion of caste as it operates in Nepal, see Fürer-Haimendorf (1957, 1959, 1960, 1966).

4. See Fürer-Haimendorf 1956; Rosser 1966.

5. See Chapter 3.

6. See Tucci 1962.

7. See Hamilton 1819.

8. A few rajahs retained the power to collect taxes and hear certain disputes up to 1960.

9. Friendships between high castes and untouchables are by no means unknown in Nepal; indeed, there is a ritual friendship *(mit)* which can be used to cement a relationship between two persons of different or the same caste (Okada 1957; Hitchcock 1966, pp. 66–68).

10. Strictly speaking, the Giris should be regarded as a caste, not a clan, but as the villagers point out, to be a Giri (or a Puri, or Sanyasi, or any of the other ten branches of this group) is "like belonging to a clan". In Duari, the Giris have the major characteristics of a high-caste clan, in that they form a named, exogamous, residential unit with a common household god. Hence for convenience, they will be referred to as a high-caste clan, along with the Adikaris and Burtels.

11. Chetris who are descended from Brahmin or Jaisi men are referred to as Khatri Chetris. Unlike the situation in other parts of Nepal, there is no status difference in this area between Khatri Chetris and "pure" Chetris, and the two categories intermarry freely.

12. *Guthi* is land attached to a religious institution such as a temple; theoretically, it should not be sold or alienated (Regmi 1963, pp. 27–29).

2. Village Economy: Resources

Agriculture

The vast majority of people in Duari depend upon agriculture for a livelihood. The main crops are rice, grown on irrigated lands near rivers or streams, and maize, wheat, and millet, grown mainly in the dry fields on the upper part of the ridge. In addition, marrows, pumpkins, and other vegetables are grown in gardens attached to the houses.

Agricultural techniques are fairly simple. In the case of rice, the terraced fields are ploughed by a man using two bullocks and a metal-tipped wooden plough, as soon as the first rains of the monsoon begin in June. Rice seeds are then sown and left to grow to a height of a few inches. The seedlings are transplanted from the seed beds to the rest of the fields by teams of women, while the men continue to prepare the land which is about to be planted. This is a period when large aggregates of labourers are required, and each household has to recruit extra help. While the rice is growing, it requires two weedings; this job is also performed by women. Finally, it is harvested in the autumn by members of both sexes and laid out in the fields to dry in the sun. Most rice is threshed on the spot by teams of bullocks before being carried hundreds of feet up the steep mountainsides to the houses. The cultivation of rice, more than of any other crop, calls for a large amount of co-operation, not only in making up labour teams, but also in the use of scarce irrigation channels, particularly around transplanting time. Quarrels over water rights are frequent at this time of year.

Maize is planted in dry fields, which have been ploughed, and, like rice, it ripens over the summer. Wheat is grown in the same fields during the winter. In order to support two crops, the land must be fertilised with a mixture of cattle dung and green leaves, which is ploughed into the ground before each sowing. On the whole, the cultivation of dry fields requires much less work than that of rice fields. Furthermore, much of it can be done by women. Thus, after the rice harvest, men are free to leave the village; some go in search of work in India and others to buy imported goods in the terai.

Households

A household, which may occupy only part of a dwelling or, as in a few instances, more than one dwelling, is the basic economic unit in Duari. It is not, however, an easy unit to identify. In Duari, there are households which may be clearly classified as joint (that is, they contain two or more married couples), just as there are households which are clearly of the nuclear type. But there are many which cannot be readily allocated to either category. One of the difficulties is that it may be in a process of transformation from one to the other, a process which can last for several years.

Frequently, when a young man is first married, his wife does not come to live with him but remains in her natal home. When she reaches puberty, she joins her husband's household, although she may not sleep with him. Later, the son may request separate sleeping arrangements for himself and his wife and may be granted space under the eaves. The next stage is often the building of a separate cooking hearth for the young couple, but it may be some time before the son is able to persuade his father to give him his share of the family land and to register it in his name at the treasury office. The final stage comes when the young couple can afford to build its own house, and by this time the land will certainly have been divided up, and worked, and its produce consumed separately. However, it often happens that, while some sons separate completely, others remain attached to the parental household—perhaps, each with a room of his own and a separate cooking hearth, but all working their father's land together.

What must be emphasized is that there is no strict rule about the division of a joint household, nor is it marked by a formal ceremony. For the villagers, there is no one moment in time when a son becomes separate from his father; rather, it is viewed as a process. At any moment, a man may claim to be separate from his father, when he merely means that he and his wife occupy their own part of the house, while his father will maintain that his son is certainly not separate. No single criterion is universally used, although such considerations as separate sleeping arrangements and cooking hearths, the person in whose name the land is registered, and the person(s) actually working the land are all important.

I have taken the division of land as the paramount criterion, and on this basis there are 248 separate households in Duari.[1]

A household is classified as joint when two or more married males live in it with their wives, all working the same, undivided land. The men concerned may be father and son or brothers. Under this definition, just over one-fifth of the households in Duari (22.6 percent of high-castes, and 20 percent of untouchables) may be classified as joint. Table 4 shows the distribution of joint and nuclear households by caste.

TABLE 4. JOINT AND NUCLEAR HOUSEHOLDS IN DUARI (by Caste).

caste	number of households	nuclear households	joint households
Jaisi	77	63 (81.8%)	14 (18.2%)
Brahmin	35	26 (74.2%)	9 (25.8%)
Chetri	7	5 (71.4%)	2 (28.6%)
Giri	5	2 (40%)	3 (60%)
TOTAL HIGH-CASTE	124	96 (77.5%)	28 (22.5%)
Cobbler	112	90 (80.3%)	22 (19.7%)
Tailor	8	6 (75%)	2 (25%)
Smith	4	3 (75%)	1 (25%)
TOTAL UNTOUCHABLE	124	99 (79.9%)	25 (20.1%)
TOTAL HOUSEHOLDS	248	195 (78.6%)	53 (21.4%)

The average size of a household in the village is five persons, and, on the whole, there is no great difference in size between households of high-castes and of untouchables. Brahmin households, however, are the largest, with an average of six persons in each, partly because more of them are joint, and partly because Brahmin men have a higher polygyny rate than men of other castes.

When married men continue to live in their fathers' households, it is usually because they thus derive certain benefits, generally economic.[2] In Duari, those households with the largest land holdings, who gain by working them co-operatively, tend to remain together. Poorer households, which have less land and rely on other sources, such as agricultural labour, for their living, derive little benefit from living together and tend to break up. Joint households, then, are particularly useful to Brahmins.[3] There are two major reasons for this. The first is that Brahmins are precluded by their caste status from ploughing. Most Brahmin households therefore keep an untouchable ploughman, who is paid a fairly standard grain wage, regardless of how much land he helps to cultivate. Obviously, it is more economical for a large household to employ one man, than for several smaller units to engage several ploughmen.

Secondly, people living in joint households are more often able to pursue other interests away from the land. Brahmin priests are frequently called away to serve their clients in other villages. Until recently, it was also mainly Brahmins who held civil-service or teaching posts outside the village, and, of course, this was made easier by living in joint households.

It may be asked whether the fact that the majority of villagers now live in simple households is symptomatic of social change. On the whole, this does not seem likely; from personal histories collected, it appears that men now in middle life separated from their fathers in their early twenties, if they were going to separate at all before their deaths, just as they do today. Recent land-reform legislation may be affecting partition decisions in some wealthy families. A few

Brahmin and Jaisi households have broken up since the introduction of the 1964 land-reform programme, which lays down a ceiling on the amount of land to be held by any one household. This apart, however, it does not seem that economic change and, in particular, greater monetisation, has affected the domestic cycle or the incidence of joint households, as it has been observed to do in parts of India (See Epstein 1962).

Before discussing the economic categorisation of households, I would point out that a decision to partition a household does not always mean a final and complete break. Where partition has been accompanied by bitter quarrelling, the couple going off generally builds its own house away from the parental house. But in most instances sons remain close to their fathers, and frequently agnates form clusters of houses. Such proximity of residence usually indicates close co-operation in many spheres, particularly in working the land. A man will look after his brother's land while he takes a government job or, as happens frequently among untouchables, while he goes to India for a short time in search of work. I even came across instances where brothers who have separated into simple households have pooled their resources for a period while one of them was away.

Co-operation between the former members of a single household is shown not only during the absence of one of their number, but also in the help each provides the other during the agricultural season. The first helpers to be called to assist in a rice transplanting operation *(ropai)* are brothers' families. Usually brothers plan the dates for their transplantings together, to make sure that there is no overlapping. Some brothers also share a pair of bullocks, since the cost of a good animal is high.

Economic Classification of Households

Every household in Duari owns some land, even if it is very little. A household head, when asked for his occupation, will reply that he is a farmer, even though he might own a shop or hold a civil-service post, be a priest, or practice some craft. It is thus useful initially to classify households into categories on the basis of grain production in relation to size.[4]

By considering the number of consumption-units[5] in each household, rather than the number of persons, we can distinguish three major categories of household: those which produce surpluses of grain over food needs, those which have just sufficient, and those which do not produce enough. The last category, which is also the largest, may be further sub-divided, for clarity, into those producing half their needs or more and those producing less than half. These categories approximate very closely the caste divisions in the village, as Table 5 shows.

TABLE 5. ADEQUACY OF GRAIN PRODUCTION OF HOUSEHOLDS IN DUARI.

Caste	Category A (surplus)	Category B (sufficient)	Category C1 (deficient but more than half of need)	Category C2 (deficient less than half of need)
Jaisi	20 %	20 %	53 %	6 %
Brahmin	29.4%	14.7%	44 %	12 %
Chetri	28.6%	28.6%	28.6%	14.3%
Giri	___	___	100 %	___
TOTAL HIGH-CASTE	22 %	18 %	53 %	8 %
Cobbler	1.6%	1.6%	42.7%	54 %
Tailor			50 %	50 %
Smith	___	___	75 %	25 %
TOTAL UNTOUCHABLE	1.5%	1.5%	44 %	53 %

NOTE. These figures involve the total amount of grain yielded by the land worked by each household. Grain income from other sources is not included.

The vast majority of untouchable households (97 percent) do not produce enough grain to meet their annual food needs, whereas only 61 percent of high-caste households fall into this category. Furthermore, the majority of untouchable households produce less than half of their requirements. This disparity is a result of the unequal distribution of land. Most people work the land they own and have relatively few opportunities to gain the use of other lands, although this does sometimes happen, as when land is share-cropped or taken under mortgage *(mat bandhaki)*. Brahmins own a great deal of the land and also gain the use of the lands of other castes—mostly untouchables—through mortgages. Share-cropper tenants are generally Jaisis, more rarely, untouchables, and they work the land of rich Brahmins or Jaisis. It is therefore difficult for untouchables to obtain extra land to cultivate, and some do not even have the use of their own lands because they are mortgaged to Brahmins.

This disparity in land resources, measured by household production, can be demonstrated also by comparing the members of each caste as a proportion of the village population with the proportion of the total amount of grain produced by each caste, as in Table 6.

TABLE 6. ANNUAL PRODUCTION OF EDIBLE GRAIN IN DUARI (BY CASTE).

caste	number of members	percentage of village population	muris produced	percentage of village production
Jaisi	371	30.0	855.5	47.6
Brahmin	181	14.6	419.3	23.3
Chetri	43	5.0	53.8	3.0
Giri	28	2.1	50.0	2.8
TOTAL HIGH-CASTE	623	51.7	1378.6	76.7

Table 6. (CONT'D)

caste	number of members	percentage of village population	muris produced	percentage of village production
Cobbler	529	42.3	349.5	19.4
Tailor	50	3.9	29	1.6
Smith	21	1.7	25	1.4
TOTAL UNTOUCHABLE	600	47.9	403.5	22.4

While untouchables comprise nearly half the village population, they produce less than a quarter of the annual grain harvest; whereas the high-castes, who constitute just over half the population, produce rather more than three-quarters of the grain. An additional factor is that in Tables 5 and 6, only grain produced in Duari has been taken into account. Six Brahmin households own land either in a valley south of Belaspur District or in the terai, which together produce an additional two hundred *muris* of grain annually. This land is worked by tenants on a share-cropping basis (*adyan*, or half to the tenant and half to the owner). Allowing for the tenants' share of the produce this still means an extra hundred muris, or about 25 percent of the production by Brahmin households on village lands. When this is added to their previous figures, the Brahmins are shown to produce an even higher proportion of grain.

There is also some disparity in grain production among the high-caste clans, although it is not as glaring as that between high-castes and untouchables. Using the same categories as in Table 5, but substituting high-caste clans for castes, as in Table 7, we find that the Ramas tend to be better off than the other high-caste clans, except for the small Burtel clan of six households, half of which have surpluses.

TABLE 7. ADEQUACY OF
GRAIN PRODUCTION OF HIGH-CASTE HOUSEHOLDS (by Clan).

clan	number of households	category A	category B	category C1	category C2
Rama	57	31.6%	7.0%	47.3%	14.0%
Naule	25	24	24.0	32.0	16.0
Adikari	24	16.6	8.3	37.5	37.5
Burtel	6	50		16.6	33.2
Giri	5	0		80.0	20.0

KEY. For definitions of categories, see Table 5.
NOTE. Seven households belonging to "other" high-caste clans (see Table 3, note 4) are ignored here.

Two major points emerge from this discussion. The first is that there is a very large disparity in the amount of grain produced by various households. The high castes, on the whole, produce considerably more proportionately than the untouchables, and certain high-caste clans produce more than others. The second point is that most households do not produce sufficient grain for their food needs.[6]

Before I go on to discuss these points, the extent of the deficit will need to be clarified.

The Grain Deficit

Village lands *in toto* produce just over half (54 percent) of the grain needed to feed the population. It is generally agreed by the villagers that this deficit is a recent phenomenon and that one or two generations ago far fewer persons were using the same amount of land. Some idealise the past and claim that "in those days, everyone had enough land". This is probably not entirely correct, although it is possible that the land was somewhat more equitably distributed. What seems indisputable is that the population is increasing at such a rate that there is acute pressure on the land.

In the Belaspur treasury tax records of twenty-seven years ago, ninety-five houses were registered in the village. Today, there are more than double that number. Even allowing for possible inaccuracies in the records, it seems likely that the number of households has increased considerably, and, as has been shown, not because of any sudden increase in the partitioning of joint households or because of any more immigration. The reason is the high birth-rate.

As might be expected in such a remote and undeveloped area, the infant-mortality-rate is high and life-expectancy very low. A large number of children die before the age of five years—according to my census, at least a third of those born alive. There is a high incidence of tuberculosis and other respiratory diseases, dysentery of various kinds, debilitation due to internal parasites, and all the consequences of a diet which is frequently deficient in certain vitamins and minerals and which in some cases, particularly of poor untouchables, lacks sufficient calories.[7]

In 1969 a census was made of the total number of children born to men then more than sixty years old—that is, of men who can reasonably be expected not to have any more children.[8] In spite of high infant mortality, such men had produced an average of four children who had survived to the age of marriage. Land is divided equally among a man's sons (daughters only inheriting in exceptional circumstances), so, assuming a roughly equal proportion of males to females,[9] the land of an average household must be divided into at least two parts each generation. This process has probably been going on for some time, since there have been no new medical facilities in the area which might have led to an increase in the number of children surviving. Recently, the situation of the grain deficit has become serious because there is no new land to cultivate and no new techniques for increasing yield, nor does emigration offer a valid solution. A generation ago, the village was probably just sufficient in grain; two generations ago, it may even have produced a surplus, although it is likely that slightly less land was then under cultivation. Today, the land produces only half the population's grain requirements, and the population appears to be doubling each generation.

The Need for Cash

Even before pressures on the land became acute and the village ceased to be self-sufficient in grain, certain commodities were required which were not produced, or even available, locally. The most important of these, cloth, was brought to the hills from India via the terai. Another, salt, was traditionally bought from passing traders or in the terai. Cash was required to acquire both these commodities and to pay land taxes.

Today, cash is needed even more. Cloth and salt are still bought for, and taxes paid in cash; but now villagers also need to import grain, some of which is paid for in cash. In addition, new consumer goods are in increasing demand—tea, sugar, soap, and pens, to name a few. Moreover, cash is increasingly required not only to pay for the greater range and quantity of imported goods, but also to pay for goods and services available locally. The importance of cash in the economy today can best be illustrated by considering some household budgets. In a small sample of twelve households of all the major castes (Brahmin, Jaisi, Cobbler, and Tailor), it was found that the minimum amount of cash needed annually was 1,000 rupees ($100, at the 1969 rate of exchange) and that some households claimed to spend as much as 4,000 rupees (about $400).

Questions were asked about cash spent in the past twelve months on foods other than grain, tobacco, jajmani services, other services (for example, agricultural labour), cloth, festivals, taxes, and school fees. In addition, questions were asked about major items of expenditure over the previous three years, such as animals, land, rituals like weddings and funerals, and house-building; these were converted into an annual average. The sample of household budgets is summarised in Table 8.[10]

TABLE 8. AVERAGED ANNUAL CASH EXPENDITURES OF TWELVE DUARI
HOUSEHOLDS ON ITEMS OTHER THAN GRAIN.

item	rupees per consumption-unit[1]		percentage of averaged expenditures	
	high-caste	untouchable	high-caste	untouchable
food (other than grain)	146.18	62.36	23.6	25.8
tobacco	40.36	23.63	6.5	9.8
cloth	100.36	47.63	16.2	19.7
services	40.64	5.81	6.5	2.4
taxes	9.82	1.27	1.6	.5
festivals	46.60	29.45	7.5	12.2
miscellaneous	52.90	6.18	8.5	2.6
non-recurrent major items	183.80	65.45	29.6	27
TOTAL	620.66	241.78	100.0	100.0

1. The use of consumption units, rather than persons or households seems more useful in this context, just as it was in estimating amounts of grain needed per household in Table 5.

As the sample is so small, households have only been categorised into high-caste and untouchable. Both categories include joint and simple households.

Food: Cash spent on foods other than grain tends to vary according to caste status. On the whole, high-caste households spend more on luxury foods such as tea, sugar, and meat than do untouchable households. One Jaisi in the sample, who has a government job and whose land produces sufficient grain, spends 10 rupees each month on meat, while the poorest untouchable family in the sample barely manages to buy meat twice a year, for the two major religious festivals of Dasein and Tiwar.

Tobacco: This is a considerable item in the budgets of nearly all households. On the whole, persons who are primarily farmers, who visit the bazaar comparatively seldom, often grow their own tobacco, and therefore need little cash. But people who work in the bazaar or visit it regularly prefer manufactured cigarettes imported from the *terai;* this applies equally to high-castes and untouchables.

Cloth: Expenditure on cloth varies directly according to caste status. The least is spent by Cobblers, who are not expected to dress well even when they visit the bazaar. Members of high-castes who have jobs in the bazaar tend to spend a lot of money on cloth, and most high-caste men attach great importance to buying good cloth for their wives. Brahmin women usually wear Indian-type silk saris for festivals and rituals, whereas other women will wear their newest cotton skirts.

Most respondents said they usually bought their cloth in the terai and then had it made up by their Tailors in the village. However, when asked where they had bought cloth for specific items of clothing in the past year, the majority were found to have made their purchases in Belaspur Bazaar. An extra incentive to buying cloth in the bazaar, despite higher prices, is the fact that credit can often be obtained there; more people buy for cash than credit, however.

Services: Money spent on services also varies according to caste. Untouchables do not have the services of Brahmin priests. At weddings and funerals a real or classificatory son-in-law acts as a priest and receives a little money for it. But Brahmin priests who serve the high castes receive large payments in cash and goods for all types of rituals and, in addition, are given regular "charity". High-caste people spend varying amounts on their priests during an average year, the amount usually ranging between 50 and 100 rupees in cash, as well as grain and other goods. If a wedding or, especially, a funeral takes place, then the amount would be very much more.

Tailors and Smiths receive very much less from their clients than do priests. They are paid mostly in grain at the time of harvest, but in addition they may receive a rupee or two in cash at the time of important festivals. A few poor untouchables, and even some high-caste households, do not have jajmani relationships with Tailors or Smiths, but pay in cash for each item made. They reckon this to be cheaper than having to pay a fixed amount of grain, although it does reflect on their status. Tailors and Smiths exchange services with one another, without any grain or cash changing hands.

It is interesting to note that all the households sampled claim to spend money on employing agricultural labour. The high-caste households, of course, spend much more, but even the poorest Cobbler household pays out a few rupees in cash to obtain all the help needed. This is strongly illustrative of the trend toward the greater monetisation of the economy. People now prefer to work for cash whenever they can, even in situations where they would previously have exchanged labour with fellow-caste-members.

TAXES: Taxes on lands and households form a very small percentage of annual expenditure. However, land in the plains and valleys to the south is very heavily taxed, so the six Brahmin households owning land in these areas—one of which appears in the sample—pay large amounts of tax. However, they are all wealthy, and land taxes remain a fairly small proportion of their annual expenses. School fees are likewise not high, but most parents are deterred from sending their children to school by the cost of books and respectable clothes, not to mention their reluctance to lose the children's labour.

FESTIVALS: The most important festivals celebrated by the villagers are Dasein and Tiwar. At these times, extra luxury food is purchased, and untouchables make large supplies of liquor *(rakshi)*. The annual supply of new clothes is generally purchased and worn at this time.

MISCELLANEOUS: This category includes such items as soap, medicines, books, stationery, kerosene, shaving equipment, and padlocks. Very few such goods are bought by untouchables. All, with the exception of some locally produced medicines, are imported items, usually made in India and purchased in Belaspur Bazaar, where they are relatively expensive.

NON-RECURRENT ITEMS: During the three years investigated, almost every household in the sample had needed to spend money on some sort of ceremony—funeral, wedding, naming, or house-blessing. Untouchables spend much money on weddings, with much feasting and gifts of clothing and jewellery to the bride, as well as brideprice to her parents. High-caste households, on the other hand, may spend rather less nowadays, because they still marry off their children before puberty, which is against the law. Their weddings tend therefore to be small affairs, to avoid attracting the attention of the police. With funerals, however, the reverse applies. High-caste people observe thirteen days of pollution following a death and have to make heavy payments to their priests, whereas untouchables need only mourn for three or four days, and give very little to their officiants.

Another major non-recurrent expenditure is on animals. Few untouchables buy buffaloes, partly because of their cost (around 600 rupees), but also because they bring poor returns—no high-caste man will buy dairy products from an untouchable, and few untouchables can afford to do so. Untouchables prefer to invest in bullocks when they have cash, for they can be hired out together with their owner to work in the fields of rich men. But even then, untouchables buy older, and so, less expensive, animals than members of high castes.

The latter are also the only ones to make useful long-term investments, such

A Duari priest gives tikas *(ritual marks) to his family at the festival of Dasein.*

as buying land, lending out money for interest, or stocking shops. One Brahmin in the sample bought some land outside the district for 5,000 rupees; since the land was very fertile, he could expect to recoup his costs within a few years by selling the produce.

Unfortunately, Table 8 does not include cash spent on staples—primarily grain —because it proved very difficult to estimate the cash expenditure of untouchables on this item. High-caste households with grain deficits buy their grain in bulk, usually once or twice a year, and can estimate fairly accurately how much cash they might need to cover this item. It is usually a fairly small amount, averaging 48 rupees per consumption-unit. Untouchables need a great deal more grain to make up their larger deficits, but they obtain it, as will be shown, in various ways—by borrowing, by working for grain, and by buying in small quantities—which makes the amount hard to calculate.

Some households do not spend any money on buying grain; these include both Brahmin and Tailor households. Even if such a household has a deficit, it is made up by grain given by clients in return for caste-specific services.

Summary

High-castes spend more on each item, in terms of cash, than do untouchables, although proportions spent on different items tend not to vary much according to caste. Staples apart, high-caste households spend more than do untouchable households.

This discussion of household budgets, even though it is based on a small sample, does reveal a number of points: One is the importance of cash in the economy; with the exception of grain, most household needs must be met by cash. The second is the difference in the styles of living of high-castes and untouchables. The former spend more per household and per consumption-unit on items which all need to buy and, in addition, spend on a wider range of items, particularly luxury goods; they also spend more on non-recurrent expenses and can afford to invest, as well.

In sum, then, we have a situation in which the village as a whole is deficient in grain; many households do not produce enough for their needs, and there is a wide disparity in grain-incomes. The economy is one in which cash is increasingly used for a wide range of goods and services, although it must be borne in mind that cash has been needed for essential imported goods and for taxes for a long time. How the grain deficit is made up, and where the villagers obtain their cash will be explored in the next chapter.

NOTES

1. I have been able to do this because, with a single exception, mentioned in Chapter 6, there are no landless households in Duari.

2. Berreman (1963, p. 147) notes that "larger joint families are usually retained when it is advantageous or necessary to do so, and they break down more readily when they perform no useful or necessary function".

3. However, in a comparative study of twenty-six villages in India, Kolenda found that Brahmins tended to live less often in joint families than did other castes (1968, p. 390). This may be accounted for by the fact that Brahmins were not necessarily the wealthiest castes in these villages.

4. It is not useful to consider the area of land held by each household. First, because several different measures of land exist in western Nepal, which makes for confusion. Second, terraces on steep mountainsides do not lend themselves to accurate measurement. Third, the land itself is of such variable quality that production fluctuates enormously. The grains considered are rice, wheat, maize, and a little millet and barley, which is grown by a minority of people. It is generally reckoned locally that paddy yields 50 percent of its weight in edible grain (rice), wheat yields 100 percent of its weight in flour, and maize (off the cob) yields 100 percent. My figures, then, are for net edible grains in 1969, a year of average harvest.

5. One consumption-unit requires 4½ *muris,* (1 *muri*-160 pounds) of edible grain per annum or two pounds per day. One consumption-unit is reckoned as a person over 14 years of age; a child aged 9–14 is half a unit; a child aged 3–9

is a quarter of a unit. Children under three years old are discounted.

6. Duari is not atypical in this respect. Cool (1967, p. 12) notes: "With the exception of Tibrikot district, all the Far Western Hills districts are foodgrain deficit areas. The annual deficit in the remaining 17 districts has been estimated at approximately 76,000 metric tons of foodgrain".

7. Worth and Shah (1969, p. 43) also found a much higher incidence of malnutrition among untouchables than among high-castes.

8. It might have been more satisfactory to consider the number of children born to all village women, but a detailed census of the female population was much more difficult to carry out than of the male particularly because the assistants used had to be male. In any case, it may be more useful to consider children in relation to males in this context, since men remain in the village, whereas women marry out and frequently change their villages of residence after divorce or widowhood, and because men own the land, which is divided among their sons.

9. The average number of sons born to these men is 2.19 and of daughters, 1.71.

10. It must be noted that these figures are estimates given by household heads (sometimes with their wives) and there is some likelihood of exaggeration, or at least a tendency to state the ideal. The main purpose of these figures is to indicate the importance of cash in the economy and to demonstrate the differences in the ways it is spent by high-castes and untouchables.

3. The Village Economy: Earning a Living

People work both inside and outside the village for cash and grain. Formerly, work in the village was rewarded by grain, and cash had to be earned elsewhere, often far afield, as the district economy generated very little. Over a period of time, cash has come more and more to be available nearer at hand; it can now be earned in the bazaar and even within the village.

Jajmani-type Relationships

The system known as jajmani, which is such a conspicuous feature of village life in India, operates in only a limited way in Duari, as in most of the Himalayan Hills (see Berreman 1960, 1962, 1963, 1970). This is partly because only a few castes are represented in western Nepal, and numerous tasks which would in India be performed by specialists are here carried out by anyone. In the Belaspur area, there are no Barbers or Washermen, to name but two of the castes considered indispensable farther south. The word *jajman,* itself, is restricted in use in western Nepal to mean the client of a Brahmin priest. But jajmani-type relationships have traditionally existed among other castes, as well, notably between members of high castes and Tailors and Smiths; service castes in this part of Nepal refer to their clients as *bista.*

The Smiths in Duari, like the Cobblers, mostly do not perform their caste-specific occupations (those for which their caste is named), so people obtain their tools from some Smiths who live in Toli. But all the Tailors in Duari are engaged in making clothes, and all have permanent jajmani relationships with both high-caste and other untouchable households. Each of the nine Tailor households has an average of nearly thirty client households. Employers give their Tailors fixed amounts of grain annually, and the Tailors, in return, sew as many clothes as are required. Tailors normally get around five *pathis* of paddy (about 20 pounds of rice), the same quantity of maize, four pathis of wheat (32 pounds of flour) and a little millet and barley. These amounts are given at harvest-time. In addition, at the two major festivals of Dasein and Tiwar each household usually gives its Tailor a rupee in cash and a little rice. A pound of rice may also be given with each large item of work.

The Tailors are the most prosperous of the untouchable castes in the village.

31

They do not own a great deal of land, but they derive a fair income from their clients, receiving more grain than their own land produces, and, indeed, often more than they can consume by themselves. Each Tailor household owns a sewing machine, and both men and women work. Some men go to the terai for the winter to work for cash. Tailors are often in a position to lend out small amounts of cash or grain in the village.

The Brahmins also earn their living partly by caste-specific work. All the male adults of this caste work as family priests, and their clients are scattered over a very wide area. Most Brahmins have large numbers of client households, which is not surprising, considering the ratio of Brahmins to other clean castes in Belaspur District (see Table 1). Some Brahmins have as many as sixty client households, others as few as ten; the average is around twenty-five.

Priests are essential at most life-cycle ceremonies and on numerous other occasions, such as the building of new houses and calendrical rites and festivals. They receive cash and grain and other goods at all the rituals they perform. In addition, they receive "charity" on certain days of the month, or any time a client wants to acquire merit. The richer the household, the more a priest will benefit, particularly at a funeral, when the clients will do their best to give a cow, as well as other goods, to their priest. The average annual cash income from priestly services is around 3,000 rupees, but priests with many clients, or especially rich ones, would earn more. Priests inherit clients from their fathers, and they can also seek them out. In exceptional cases, a client may change his priest. Duari Brahmins serve the bazaar, which has a relatively wealthy population of government servants and shopkeepers; it is the Ramas who take their clients from this area, so it is little wonder that the Brahmin members of this clan are among the richest men in the village.

Brahmins, then, are in a fortunate position, and for a long time they have been able to command a cash income even when cash was very scarce, because many of them had clients with cash incomes—government servants, shopkeepers, or Gurkha pensioners. This they invested in land or in lending cash out for high rates of interest or land mortgages. Furthermore, most Brahmins also have surplus grain, for even if the produce of their own lands places them in a deficit category, grain given by their clients more than covers their food needs.

Plough-service

Brahmins in western Nepal do not plough fields and so must employ someone else to do the task.[1] Normally this is an untouchable, and there is a special type of relationship, known as *hali-riti* (ploughman-master), in which the landowner —in Duari, usually a Brahmin—lends the ploughman—generally a Cobbler—a sum of money (between 100 and 200 rupees), and the latter agrees to work as the former's ploughman until the loan is repaid. No interest is charged on the loan, and, in addition, the ploughman receives two or three *muris* of paddy and perhaps another *muri* of wheat, maize, and millet.[2] The ploughman is also fed on the days he works for his master. Some ploughmen work only at ploughing time, but others do much of their masters' other agricultural work, as well, and reckon to spend half their working time this way. Because the loans are large, it is often difficult for a ploughman to repay his debt, and so he is, in effect, bound to work for the landowner indefinitely. There is little chance of his borrowing a larger sum from another landowner to repay the first, and then working for the second, meanwhile retaining the incremental loan (as happens among the Limbus in east Nepal (Caplan 1970), because there are many more Cobblers in the village than Brahmins. A few Cobblers work for rich Jaisis, particularly those with government jobs, who have little time to look after their fields, and some work for wealthy non-Brahmins in nearby villages. On the whole, however, there is little demand for ploughmen by people other than Brahmins.

Cobblers who become ploughmen find a good deal of security in the arrangement. Not only are they assured of a substantial amount of grain—usually more than they get from their own lands—but they can count on their masters for advances of grain and small interest-free cash loans to meet special contingencies such as deaths in the family. They also usually get help of other kinds, such as support in minor disputes and assistance in dealing with government agencies.

The ploughman-master relationship is thus a corollary of the caste system, which stipulates that Brahmins may not plough, and of the unequal division of land and of grain production, which means that some households (usually Brahmin) require assistance of this kind, while other households (usually Cobbler) must provide it.

It is difficult to know how long this relationship has been a feature of life in the village. There are comparable institutions throughout much of north India (see Lynch 1969; Neale 1962; Cohn 1955), but it may be a fairly recent development in Duari. Village legends speak of some of the untouchables as *karia,* or people who were likely to be called on to help high-castes in times of need and who were rewarded in grain. But until the early part of this century slaves were kept by some wealthy households. The ploughman-master system, as it now operates, probably became more widespread after the abolition of slavery in 1924 and was encouraged by the growing poverty of the Cobblers, as they continued to lose much of their land to the Brahmins.

However, the most recent trend is toward a decline in the system, brought about by several factors. Many Brahmins claim that they can no longer afford to keep ploughmen; it is cheaper to hire labourers on a daily basis for cash. Second, landowners have also been discouraged by the effects of the land-reform laws passed since the revolution. Many ploughmen have had their debts cancelled under these laws after many years of service, much to the anger of their masters.

Third, untouchables may not care to work as ploughmen, since it takes up a lot of time which can nowadays be used in earning cash. Also, ploughmen are paid in grain, and untouchables prefer cash wages, which they can spend where and how they please. As will be shown, this often means buying the grain they need in areas outside the district, where it is relatively cheap.

Thus, at present only about half of the Brahmin households and a handful of wealthy Jaisis, use ploughmen. A few other Cobblers work as ploughmen in nearby villages for wealthy Thakuris and Chetris. The total number of Cobblers employed in this way is now only twenty-five, whereas previously, when all Brahmin households had ploughmen, the number was substantially higher.

Other Services

There are a variety of specialists in the village, such as astrologers and shamans, who can earn small amounts of cash or grain for their services. Astrologers are generally Jaisis. They have to be literate to cast horoscopes, but they are paid very little for their services, and the half-dozen men practising astrology in the village are not particularly wealthy.

Shamans can be of any caste from Brahmin to Cobbler, and they are usually male. They are possessed by those gods which are worshipped as household deities in Duari. Usually a shaman is possessed by his own household god, but this is not always the case; one Naule shaman is possessed by the household god of the Adikaris, as is a Cobbler shaman. Shamans also function as diviners and curers, and in this society they work in cooperation with Brahmin priests.[3] They tend to be paid very little and to have no particular influence.

In contrast to shamans and astrologers, a specialist who makes quite a large income is a case-writer *(lekhendas)*. In a society where disputes—particularly over land—are frequent and many are brought to government offices such as the treasury or the land-reform office, as well as the court, the importance of being able to prepare written cases or petitions cannot be overestimated.[4] Most villagers, even the literate ones, also require help in coping with the many documents which accompany any dealings with the administration, because the type of Nepali which appears on most official forms is practically a different language from ordinary spoken or written Nepali; it contains a large amount of Sanskrit and many peculiar abbreviations and constructions. Writers are men of importance and influence, and two of the men who have held high office in the village are writers.

Unskilled Labour

Most people who need extra grain or cash work as unskilled labourers in Duari or nearby villages. The majority are Cobblers or Smiths or, more occasionally, poorer Jaisis and Chetris; usually they perform agricultural work, but they may also build or repair houses or cattle sheds.

Agricultural labourers, both men and women, are generally needed at peak times, such as paddy transplanting, and harvesting. The wages in Duari are 2 rupees plus a meal daily, or else one pathi (about 8 pounds) of paddy (which makes 4 pounds of rice) and a meal. Frequently, grain is borrowed in advance against a promise to do a day's work at a later date. It seems likely that until recently agricultural labourers were paid in grain. Today, they are more likely to be paid in cash. In a survey of twenty-five transplantings during the monsoon of 1969, I found that, although the majority of helpers were not paid labourers (that is, they were either members of the household or people with whom reciprocal labour arrangements had been made), those who were working for wages were more likely to be paid in cash than kind. Those who were working for grain had generally received it in advance in the form of loans.

Animal Husbandry

Buffaloes, cows, bullocks, and goats are kept by members of all castes; untouchables also keep pigs and chickens. Buffaloes and cows are useful mainly for their milk, although one of the former is occasionally slaughtered as a sacrifice to a god. Goat meat is eaten by all castes. In Duari, buffalo meat, pork, chicken, and eggs are consumed only by untouchables.[5]

Buffalo milk is the main source of dairy products—curds, buttermilk, and clarified butter *(ghiu)*. The last has been an important export from the Far Western Hills to the terai for a long time (see McDougal 1968, pp. 35, 47). Until recently, there was no local market for butter; it is even said that high-caste households were forbidden to sell dairy products, which have a certain ritual value, and got around this prohibition by selling in the terai. For many years, the sale of butter has provided the cash to buy cloth and salt and to pay taxes. Today the forests, particularly around the bazaar, are considerably depleted, and the importance of butter as an export from this area would seem to be declining. Not only is less butter produced, as fewer animals can be kept, but there is a ready local market for it in Belaspur Bazaar.

Milk is not always turned into butter, but is sometimes sold immediately. Early every morning small children can be seen heading toward the bazaar with cans of milk, which they sell to government servants and tea-stall owners. Some people, however, do continue to make and accumulate butter for an annual trip to the terai, where they get a better price.

High-caste households tend to own the most cattle, with an average of over three animals per household. Untouchables, on the other hand, average fewer than two animals. Different castes tend to own different kinds of animals. The largest numbers of buffalo are owned by Jaisis, who are also the people who depend for much of their cash income on the sale of dairy products—either milk in the bazaar or butter in the terai markets. Brahmins receive some butter from their clients, so instead of buffalo, they tend to keep cows, which they also obtain from clients on the occasion of a funeral. These animals produce very little milk, but have a high ritual value. When untouchables own animals, they tend to have bullocks, which they can hire out for ploughing. They rarely own buffaloes or cows, as they cannot sell dairy products to high-castes, and fellow untouchables are unlikely to have money to buy them.

Most of these ways of earning a livelihood are not new, although until fairly recently they were more likely to be means of earning grain than cash. They were, moreover, the ways in which grain was distributed through the village population, from the wealthy to the poor. Cash was another matter; Brahmins obtained it from their clients, while non-Brahmin high-castes obtained it by selling their butter in the terai. The latter mainly spent it on the spot. Only a small amount found its way back to the district. In fact, cash was in very short supply.[6] One Cobbler told me: "In my youth, we had great trouble getting hold of cash. Not only did we do work such as portering for next to nothing, but if we were in immediate need of money, we went to a shopkeeper in the bazaar (there were probably less than a dozen shops at the time), and we gave him half a *muri* of grain for just a rupee." Today a *muri* of grain fetches 40 rupees.

However, even then, untouchables could ill spare grain to "buy" cash. Only two methods of obtaining cash were open to them: to borrow it, or to migrate to India for work.[7]

Loans

Until fairly recently, the only people in the village who had regular access to cash were Brahmins, especially Rama Brahmins, because of their work as priests in the surrounding villages, where some of their clients were Gurkha pensioners, and in the bazaar where their clients were shopkeepers and government servants. Because of the need for their services, the Brahmins were in a strong position to demand payment in cash rather than grain, even when cash was scarce. In addition, a handful of them, as long as a generation ago, held government or teaching posts for which they were paid in cash.

The Brahmins brought the cash they earned into the village and distributed much of it in the form of loans. These were of several types:

1. a loan *(rin)* carrying a fixed rate of interest, usually around 25 percent per annum, which would usually be secured by cattle or jewellery;
2. an interest-free loan *(mat bandaki)* for which land was given as security and where the creditor had the use of the land until the principal was repaid;
3. an interest-free loan for which the debtor agreed to work for the creditor until the loan was repaid (the master-ploughman (hali-riti) relationship, already discussed); and
4. a small, interest-free loan *(sapat),* usually without a written document, made for a short period to a relative or friend.

It was mainly through the giving of loans that Brahmins acquired the large amount of land they hold today. If they worked a plot of mortgaged land which was not redeemed by its owner after a considerable period, the Brahmins often had the land registered in their own names or else insisted that the land be sold outright to them, so that the debtor would have the cash to repay the loan.

Brahmins lent money to members of all castes, but it was mainly the untouchables who suffered a serious diminution in the amount of land they owned. One old Cobbler explained what had happened in this way:

The Brahmins got property from their clients and some from untouchables. In this way, they became rich. They invested their money in the village, in the form of loans, and the money increased. The untouchables couldn't meet all their cash needs, and they borrowed from rich people, and mortgaged their land, or sold it. In any case, the untouchables kept only the land which they needed at the time, and didn't think that in the future their descendants would need more land.

The same story was repeated to me time after time by untouchables: "once we owned all the land in this village; now we are poor."

Untouchables often maintain that they were tricked out of their land: "High-caste people try to take our land for less than its value. They give a loan of 100 rupees, but they make it out on paper as 1,000 rupees. Since untouchables are illiterate, they can easily be cheated. Then when the debtor asks the creditor to read the agreement to him, the latter leaves out the extra nought. And they have another trick: they refuse to give a receipt to the debtor when he comes to pay the interest. Later they claim that neither interest nor principal has ever been paid, and in this way they get our land."[8]

The Brahmins agree that they have obtained most of their lands from untouchables, particularly Cobblers, but they maintain that it was done fairly, either by buying outright, or by foreclosing on mortgages; in the latter instance, they claim that it is the fault of the untouchables for failing to pay back money borrowed.

This section, then, answers the earlier question of how the Cobblers have come to have so small a share of the village lands. The loss of their lands is the basis of the very real antagonism existing between the Cobblers and the Brahmins, especially the Rama Brahmins, who are seen as the chief culprits. This antagonism has had important political repercussions, as will be shown in Chapter 4.

Land and Credit Reform

Various post-revolutionary governments have attempted to deal with the problems of unequal distribution of land and the chronic indebtedness of peasants, many of whom own no land at all, in Nepal. A number of new laws[9] have been passed, whose provisions include:

1. a ceiling on the size of holdings by any one household and redistribution of any surplus to the landless and poor;
2. greater security for tenants;

3. abolition of the rights and privileges of such tax-collectors as the headman (mukhiya) and the senior headman (jimmawal), including their rights to corvée;

4. interception of agricultural loans by government agencies (that is, the land-reform offices which were set up throughout the country during the 1960s);

5. a maximum interest rate on loans of 10 percent per annum;

6. the setting up of a compulsory savings scheme, which would become a source of credit for all farmers.

In 1966, land reform was instituted in Belaspur District and an office set up in the bazaar. In each Administrative Village, surveys were made of the amount of land held by each household, and information about debts and loans was collected. But none of the people in Duari is satisfied with the land-reform measures.

The untouchables had expected that they would get more land from the surplus of other households, but in Duari no household held land in excess of the ceiling; the few which might have (some wealthy Rama Brahmins who own land outside the district), had rapidly partitioned their property as soon as they heard about land reform. There was thus no surplus to redistribute.

Some of the wealthier landowners who do not cultivate all their lands themselves are alarmed by measures to protect tenants. In this area, the only form of tenancy is share-cropping *(adyan),* which is practised by only a few persons in Duari. However, the practise appears to have been gaining ground in the early 1960s; some landowners have found it just as economical as to cultivate themselves, thereby having to employ a ploughman and labourers. Usually the land-owners are wealthy Brahmins or Jaisis and the tenants poor Jaisis or occasionally, Cobblers. The new legislation stipulates that tenants who cultivate the same piece of land for more than twelve months should have certain inalienable rights in it and cannot be summarily evicted. The effect of the new measures in Duari has been either to make landowners reluctant to take on tenants or to take them for very short periods, usually only one agricultural season. Neither party has found this arrangement satisfactory, and for the poorer villagers it has also eliminated a means of cultivating extra land.

The compulsory savings scheme is also highly unpopular, and most people regard it as another form of taxation. In many parts of Nepal, the scheme has proved unworkable for a number of reasons: its unpopularity, poor harvests, lack of understanding of its purposes, and the incompetence of those who are supposed to collect the savings (an example of this is given in Chapter 5). The scheme was, in fact, temporarily suspended after rioting took place in one area of Nepal in 1969.

As far as Duari villagers are concerned, the most important provisions of the land-reform acts concern debts and loans. The idea is that all borrowers and lenders should furnish the land-reform office with complete lists of their credit dealings; debts are to be verified, particularly in cases where debtor's and lender's versions conflict. Where extremely high interest-rates have been charged, some of the interest is supposed to be deducted from the principal, allowing only for 10 percent interest per annum on the original loan.

Many untouchables, particularly those deeply in debt, had hoped for great things from credit reform, but here again they have been disappointed. A Cobbler told me:

We thought that we would be better off, but things are just the same as before. Poor people were supposed to be helped, but those rich people are crafty, and they continue to deceive us. If we go and complain about them to the land-reform office, they claim that we are insulting them.

This man's grandfather had mortgaged a piece of land to one of the wealthiest Rama Brahmins in the village, who had, so the Cobbler claimed, refused to let him pay off the loan and recover his land. Since the Cobbler had no copy of the original agreement, the case has been dragging on, with the Cobbler having to go from office to office in an attempt to reclaim his land.

There was a general expectation that with the introduction of the land-reform programme all debts would be cancelled. This of course has not happened, although some people's debts have been reduced because they have been paying such high rates of interest, because they have not had the use of their lands for many years, or because they have worked as ploughmen for a long time. A few have been able to recover their lands from creditors who held them under mortgage. But most remain disappointed.

There seems little doubt that debts and loans are underreported. According to the land-reform office list of debts in Duari, sixty-eight loans are outstanding, of which forty-one (60 percent) involve mortgaged land. More loans are listed as having been made to high-caste persons than to untouchables, whereas all the evidence gathered during fieldwork suggests that far more untouchables than high-castes borrow (and lose their land through mortgaging). It is likely that untouchables do not report their loans from ignorance of their new rights, lack of documentary evidence, fear of reprisals, or general inability to cope with the machinery of complaint.

At the same time, money-lenders (the Brahmins), have been angered by many of the new measures. For the first time they find themselves to be engaged in disputes with untouchables on an equal basis, in which one of the latter occasionally wins the case. They think it unfair also that some debts should be cancelled or reduced. Most claim that the 10 percent ceiling is far too low a rate of interest and that it is now uneconomical to lend money at all. Indeed, only a few Brahmins still consider giving loans, and then only if the borrower agrees to pay the old interest-rates unofficially. It is, not unnaturally, difficult to obtain precise information on this subject, but certainly the rate of interest on grain borrowed in Duari remains 25 percent.

The general effect of the land-reform laws and their implementation in the district, then, has been to make credit much harder to obtain.[10] When loans are made, they are usually given without signed agreements and certainly not through the official channels set up by the land-reform acts.

However, the diminution of credit sources has been offset for both borrowers and lenders by new opportunities for earning cash. Brahmins can now invest in trade, particularly in shops in the district capital or in land in more productive areas outside the district. Untouchables are no longer wholly dependent upon Brahmins if they want to obtain cash locally, for there has been a great increase in the demand for unskilled labour in the area. Even before these new opportunities arose, however, there was one way in which untouchables could obtain cash to repay at least some of their debts—by migration to India.

Migration Abroad

Migration from the hills is not a practice confined to people of Belaspur District, but is a nation-wide phenomenon. Two major categories of migrant may be distinguished—men who leave to join the Indian or British armies, generally on a long-term basis, and people who look for unskilled, seasonal employment. It is usually tribal people such as Magars, Limbus, and Gurungs who comprise the first category. In some parts of Nepal, members of these groups have raised their economic status considerably by army service; in a few instances, they can even compete with members of high castes (Caplan 1970; Hitchcock 1961). But in the Far Western Hills, comparatively few serve in the military, and these are mainly Magars because members of high castes and untouchables are rarely accepted into foreign armies.[11] In Belaspur District, over half the population is, in effect, excluded from foreign military service by virtue of caste. Even so, according to the records of the Belaspur branch of the Nepal Ex-Servicemen's Association, more than 150,000 rupees flow annually into the district from pensions, alone; this figure does not include the salaries of those currently serving. In a few parts of the district populated mainly by tribals, army service is important to the economy. Prior to the growth of the bazaar and the consequent influx of money into the district, soldiers' salaries and pensions must have constituted a substantial part of the cash flowing into the area. Among the fifty households in Magargaon, which adjoins Duari, there are nineteen members of the Ex-Servicemen's Association, twelve of whom are currently receiving pensions; another twelve men are now serving in the army.

For most of Belaspur District, however, and certainly for Duari village, it is the second category of seasonal migration which is important.[12] Many men migrate for varying periods, sometimes for several years at a stretch, sometimes just for the four slack months of winter, to seek work in India. Most who go are untouchables, primarily Cobblers; nearly 70 percent of the adult male Cobblers in the village have worked in India at some time in their lives. Jaisis, Giris, and Chetris also migrate, but in much smaller numbers; only 27 percent of the adult males in these categories have ever been to India. Very few Brahmins migrate in search of work (although many of them go on pilgrimages to shrines in India); this is because of their strong economic position.

Cobblers almost always migrate for fairly long periods, averaging well over a year for each trip. Most go between the ages of twenty and thirty years and while they are still living in joint households. Only 25 percent of the trips about which I have information took place when the migrant was living in his own simple household, and, even then, arragements had to be made to leave a brother in charge of the family and land. Cobblers who do not live close by near relatives often complain that it is impossible for them to go to India.

Migrations of high-caste men show a rather different pattern. Most of them go when they are young, but some do continue to migrate after the age of thirty. Furthermore, because they usually go for short trips of less than a year, they feel able to leave their families. Half the trips are made by men who have separated from their fathers' households.

Migration is primarily a phenomenon of the past forty years. One of the very old men in the village remembers when the first migrant left; prior to that, he says, there was no need for migration—"There was plenty of land." This seems to be borne out by comparing the migration histories of senior and junior generations in the village. Almost all Cobblers under the age of sixty have been to India, most, between the ages of twenty and thirty years, but only half of the twelve men now more than sixty years old have been. It seems likely that the beginnings of migration were necessitated by the increasing losses of land by the Cobblers, through mortgaging or sales to the Brahmins. High-caste non-Brahmins, on the other hand, started going more recently; a few had only been on their first trips when they were already middle-aged.

Untouchable and high-caste migrants are usually motivated rather differently. The commonest reason given by the former is indebtedness,[13] although the needs to buy animals (especially bullocks) and cloth and to make up food deficits are also important motivations. High-caste men, on the other hand, often claim to go for no better reason than "to see new things," and not a few of them return without any savings at all. Those who do save, spend their money on cloth[14] and other basic items, as do the Cobblers. Many of the high-caste men, however, make only one trip to India in their lives, at the time of separation from their fathers' households, to earn enough to build houses of their own or to purchase necessities such as cooking pots.

Migrants generally travel in groups of kinsmen, affines, and fellow castemen, sometimes from a number of neighbouring villages. It is rare, although not unheard-of, for a high-caste man to travel with an untouchable. Most migrants walk seventy miles to the Indian border and then travel by bus and train to their final destination. Youngsters migrating for the first time often travel with "old hands," who give them help and advice. But some youths run off to India alone and against their parents' wishes; this seems to be a common way of rebelling against family authority and finding independence. In the majority of such cases, the young men do eventually come back and settle down.

Untouchable and high-caste men also have rather different work patterns. The majority of the former go to Simla in Himachal Pradesh or Almora in Uttar Pradesh, which are favoured for reasons of proximity and climate (both are "hill stations") and also because migrants know that they can find work there. Most of them work in coal depots as porters or in light-engineering factories. In one of the former a Duari villager has worked permanently for several years and can sometimes be of assistance to fellow villagers looking for jobs.

Other untouchables work on road-building on the north Indian border with Nepal. In such jobs, small groups of friends tend to remain together, sharing expenses and food. In this way, they are able to save more easily than by living alone. Men who leave their friends on arrival in India, particularly those who go to big cities such as Delhi or Calcutta, frequently fail to save any money. Most Cobblers, however, do manage to save and return after a year or more away with at least 1,000 rupees.

High-caste men often spend their time in forests in the north Indian hills felling trees (the kind of work which, incidentally, they would consider beneath their dignity in Belaspur). They tend to save much less per trip than do Cobblers and often manage to buy only some cloth on the way back. Some return with nothing at all. One old Jaisi woman whose son had just returned from India told me: "When my youngest son got back after three months away, he had not even got a penny in his pocket. He sat down outside our house, refusing to enter, and wept. I told him not to be so silly; he was in good health, even if he hadn't got any money!"

People who stay for longer periods try to keep in touch with their families by sending letters and occasional small sums of money with other migrants returning to the village. The following letter, written by a Cobbler to his wife, was delivered to her by a fellow-casteman from a neighbouring village:

Dear Hira Devi,
    I am quite well here, and I hope that God is keeping you well there. May God bless my sons and daughters, since your happiness is mine. I send greetings to my sister and her husband, and their children.
    I have sent you Rs. 18 with Karke's younger brother, Rs. 10 with Kalo, and a further Rs. 12 with Nilo. Use Rs. 10 of this money to pay off the debt to your brother.
    I shall be returning home by the 12th day of the month of Jestha [May-June]. Please greet my neighbours and those who remember me, and thank the man who reads this letter to you. Please do not worry about me, as I am quite happy here.

In fact, money sent with friends and relatives does not always reach its destination, and most migrants prefer to bring home their savings in a lump sum.

Not unnaturally, many wives and parents are reluctant for their husbands and sons to go off to India. Frequently men intend to go only for the winter season but stay for much longer. Sometimes there is no news about them for more than a year. And yet, nearly all the migrants do return. I could find examples of only around a half-dozen men in the whole village who had left for India many years ago and of whom nothing had been heard since that time. No man leaves the village intending never to return, and none ever takes wives and children with him. Permanent migration to India is not considered a way out of economic problems in the village.

Migrants have a widely varied experience in India. Some find jobs quickly and are able to save. Others have difficult times; they may lose all their savings or not find jobs and return home vowing never to go again. Others find that they must work very hard in order to save, perhaps taking two jobs at once, such as a labouring job during the day and a night watchman's post, as well. Many migrants encounter language difficulties, as not all hill people can learn sufficient Hindi to make themselves understood, although most pick it up quickly. Those who go to the plains frequently have trouble with the climate and fall sick. And many find big cities bewildering, especially the first time. One Cobbler told me: "I hardly knew where I was, everything was so big and strange. I went on walking and walking, and eventually forgot where I had started from. In a city like Bombay, you might go out with a friend, and it would be all right if you stayed together, but if you got separated, then you'd never find each other again, even if you searched all day!" The kinds of problems encountered by migrants are not surprising, when it is remembered that in Belaspur District there are no roads, no vehicles, no machinery of any kind. Some migrants, however, are attracted by city life. High-caste men, in particular, often said ruefully that they spent all the money they earned on going to the cinema and "drinking tea in tea-shops".

Migration to India is thus stimulated by the need to obtain cash which cannot be earned locally. There are increased opportunities for wage-labour in and around the village, as will be discussed, but for the present this does not seem to have affected the numbers of men going to India. Migrants explain that they prefer to go to India when they need large sums of money. Local work is sporadic, and cash earned daily tends to melt away on everyday expenses. Work in India pays slightly better, and always in cash, never in grain. It is also paid weekly or monthly, which makes it easier to save. Some migrants tell how they find "sympathetic" employers who hold their wages for them until the end of their stay and then give them all in a lump sum. (A few, however, have found that this results in their being cheated out of their money!)

Migrants do not as yet appear to have been affected by the very high unemployment in many parts of India; although a few report difficulties in finding jobs, most seem to have little trouble obtaining unskilled work. The border between India and Nepal is an open one, so no travel documents or work permits are required by the Nepalese migrants seeking jobs in India.

Another inducement, to Cobblers in particular, for continued migration must be mentioned—the opportunity for them to escape, at least temporarily, from their caste status. All Cobbler migrants change their names on arrival in India, and I have heard of Cobblers even donning the sacred thread and pretending to be of high caste.

Migration has for the past forty years played an important part in the Duari economy. It enables Cobblers to repay debts and to make up grain deficits; it enables members of all castes to purchase cloth, salt, cooking utensils, and other necessities unavailable locally. A point which should be emphasized, however, is that migration of the kind here described does not enable a man to raise his economic standing substantially, as does military service in the Gurkhas. Migrants sometimes manage to redeem mortgaged land, but only in rare instances do they buy any new land, and then only in very small amounts. Savings from migration are, in short, used on recurrent expenditure and rarely invested.

Summary

This chapter has attempted to show how cash and grain shortages have been made up for the past two generations. For at least this length of time, and possibly for longer, Duari has not been a self-sufficient economic unit. Brahmins earn a livelihood as priests in other villages and in the bazaar; and Jaisis sell their butter in the terai, and some of them migrate to India, as do the Cobblers. But, although villagers do go outside Duari to earn a living, they have traditionally brought their cash and grain back into the village, either to spend on necessities or to invest there or to exchange for other, usually caste-specific goods and services. Nor, until recently, did these ways of earning a living—even where they involved going outside the village—change the relations among the castes within the village. This has been true particularly of the relations between the Brahmins and the Cobblers. The latter have long depended upon the former for loans of grain and cash and in return have given either their lands or their services as ploughmen or agricultural labourers. It is only since the revolution that relations between these two groups have changed and the dependence of the Cobblers upon the Brahmins has lessened considerably.

NOTES

1. Brahmins in east Nepal do plough (Caplan 1970).
2. This would be about half the grain which the ploughman would consume in a year.
3. See Berreman 1964 for a discussion of relations between Brahmins and shamans in the Indian Himalayan foothills.
4. Hitchcock found a similar situation in a Magar village (1963, p. 77).
5. Members of "drinking" castes also eat these foods.
6. Cash was also earned from service in foreign armies, mainly by members of tribal groups.
7. McDougal (1968, p. 39) found this phenomenon to be widespread throughout the Far Western Hills: "An important finding of the present study is that the average household's recurrent annual expenses tend to exceed its locally derived

income. The deficit required for expenditure is made up either with income earned in the Nepal terai and India. . . . or by borrowing."

8. A similar situation exists in east Nepal, where the tribal Limbus claim that the Brahmins have tricked them out of their lands (see Caplan 1970).

9. These include the 1957 Lands Act, the 1959 Birta Reform Act (amended in 1962), the 1963 Agricultural (New Arrangements) Act, and the 1964 Lands Act.

10. Much the same situation appears to be true in nearby districts investigated by McDougal (1968, pp. 53–54).

11. A few men from Duari have served in the Nepalese army, however. They were always stationed in the bazaar, and I have included them in the category of government servants.

12. This would seem to apply to most of the Far Western Hills (see McDougal 1968).

13. A study of migration from a village in Uttar Pradesh reveals that "all the eighteen Chamars [Cobblers] who left the village did so for the repayment of debts" (Eames 1954, p. 23).

14. In 1949, the ornithologist Dillon Ripley, while travelling up the Karnali River, met hundreds of hill-dwellers on their way to India to find work for the winter. He commented, "This seems to be a real phenomenon, all these men going hundreds, sometimes thousands of miles to make enough money to buy a few bits of cloth or cooking utensils for their families at the bazaar at the foot of the hills in which they lived . . ." (1953, p. 101).

4. The Village Economy: Recent Changes

Two main factors have affected the economy of the village in the last twenty years—the growth of Belaspur Bazaar, already briefly described, and the opening up of Lakandra Valley south of Belaspur District (see Map 1). Villagers can now find work in the bazaar as civil servants; a few have taken advantage of the growth in trade to open shops; and there is a steady demand for construction workers and porters.

Prior to the revolution, Lakandra Valley, like most valleys of the western inner terai and like the outer terai bordering India, was infested with malaria. Much of its fertile land was unused, and the only human beings who appeared able to live there were the Tharus, a tribal people. There was a small trading centre, but it was built on a hillside above the valley, which at that time was a part of Belaspur District.

Since the revolution, the situation of Lakandra has changed dramatically. Malaria has been virtually eradicated as a result of a nationwide anti-malaria campaign. A market centre has been established in the valley itself, and made the capital of a new district. An airfield has been built in the valley, and shops and offices have sprung up there, just as they have in Belaspur. Land has become more valuable and sought-after, and one *bigha* (just under two acres) now costs around 2,000 rupees; however, one bigha in this area produces around thirty *muris* of paddy, a far higher yield than a comparable area in the hills. Many wealthy hill families are beginning to invest in land in Lakandra, and some are spending their winters there because it is warmer than the hills. There is also considerable demand for unskilled labour in the valley, both for construction work and for agriculture.

These new opportunities have benefited members of all castes, although in somewhat different ways. Government employment, and investment in land in Lakandra, are confined to high castes; unskilled labour in both Belaspur Bazaar and Lakandra Valley, to untouchables. A major factor in this division is literacy.

Literacy

Until 1922, there was no school in Belaspur District. Brahmin boys, and occasionally those of other wealthy high-caste families, were taught the sacred

Hindu literature and Sanskrit by their fathers or by teachers *(gurus)* who might have several pupils each. Since Nepali, like Sanskrit, is written in the *Devanagri* script, one result of this education was literacy in the vernacular, but only for the highest castes.

In 1922, a "religion and language" school *(bhasa pathsala)* was established by the government in Belaspur Bazaar and a teacher sent from Kathmandu. The curriculum, although limited by modern standards, was an improvement on the traditional education received in the home or from a guru; it included Nepali grammar, simple arithmetic, and history. Only high-caste boys were admitted, and a much higher percentage of them obtained an education than had been possible before. The villagers of Duari, like other people living in or near the bazaar, were in a favourable position to use the school's facilities, and many of them did so, particularly those living in the two wards nearest the bazaar—that is, those inhabited mainly by Ramas and Naules. In these two wards, just under 70 percent of the adult male Jaisis and all of the male Brahmins are literate, most of them through having attended the bhasa school for a time. But in the ward which lies farthest from the bazaar, the figure for literacy drops sharply; only 40 percent of the Jaisis there are literate, and there are even a few Brahmins who are barely literate.

The school, however, offered only a limited education to its students. Those who wanted to continue studying had to go outside the district. Until the revolution, only two men had succeeded in doing this, and both were Rama Brahmins from Duari village. One was the son of the headman, and the other was the headman's brother's grandson. After a period of study in Kathmandu, these two boys were admitted to Benares Hindu University to take their *madema*[1] examinations. Because of their learning, they are referred to throughout the district as "Pandit."

As I have indicated, Brahmin priests are essential to conduct family rituals—no high-caste family can be without one—but pandits are not restricted to serving jajmans in the normal way. They, and only they, are qualified to officiate at certain elaborate and expensive rites, notably the *sapta* and *nowaha* readings, which are used to demonstrate the piety of the wealthy families sponsoring them. The two Duari pandits found themselves very much in demand, for they were the only people qualified to perform such rites in the entire district; indeed, they were often called to officiate at rites sponsored by rich families outside the district The average fee earned for such a ritual would be in the vicinity of 2,000 rupees. Not unnaturally, both of these men, who came from families already wealthy, became extremely rich in their own right.

However, they not only practiced as priests; they also became teachers. After a time in outlying parts of the district, both became teachers in Belaspur Bazaar, eventually replacing the old Kathmandu Pandit at the bhasa school.

After the revolution, the bhasa school was superseded by schools run on more modern lines. There is now a high school as well as a primary school in the bazaar, and, in addition, primary schools have been established in most parts of the district, including one in Magargaon which serves the Administrative Village of which Duari is a part. As early as 1951, the Ministry of Education published an order requiring government-sponsored and government-aided schools to admit students of untouchable status. As yet, however, only a tiny minority of students in Belaspur schools are untouchables.

The Magargaon school was founded by a former Magar serviceman just after the revolution, but it did not receive government recognition or help until 1961. The teachers at this school, all ex-servicemen, are well-respected, and it is generally acknowledged that the standards are higher than at most other schools in the area. The Magar headmaster, who served in the education corps of the Gurkhas, has made it a policy to resist discrimination in his school on the basis of caste. To this end, he even encourages physical contact among the boys of differing castes during the classes in physical education.

For this reason, some high-caste men attempted to have the school closed down or to have the teachers replaced by members of high castes. They objected to their children being taught by matwalis (members of drinking castes) and mixing freely with Magar and untouchable children. Their attempts failed, and the school is being attended by children of all castes from within the Administrative Village. Some people who live nearer to the bazaar school send their children to the Magar school in preference because of its good teaching, and all untouchables who attend school go there because of alleged discrimination and harsh treatment in the bazaar school.

However, very few untouchable children attend any school; there are perhaps half-a-dozen boys, one of whom is in the high school. Indeed, there are not even many high-caste boys from Duari in school (and no girls) because people say they cannot afford the money for clothes and books and that anyway the children are needed at home. Even when children are registered, few attend regularly. Of the sixteen Duari boys registered at the high school, only four go at all regularly. Ten boys attend the bazaar primary school and another thirteen the Magar school. In short, only about 10 percent of the school-age male population is receiving any formal education, although some boys are still taught at home.

Government Employment

During the Rana period before the revolution, there was little opportunity for employment in the bazaar. A few Brahmins worked as teachers, as cooks for government officials, or as priests attached to the local militia. Even fewer of the other high castes found employment, although some did obtain jobs as messengers in administrative offices or as militiamen. Since there were few local jobs and competition for them was keen, some even went to find work in nearby districts or in the more developed terai.

After the revolution, a variety of government departments established branches in Belaspur Bazaar, so that the number of jobs in the district civil service trebled. Duari villagers have taken advantage of this increase in job opportunities, and half of all the high-caste adult men in the village have held, or are holding, government posts.

Various factors are important in causing a man to look for salaried employment. A government job, even the lowliest, carries immense prestige. Some people state frankly that they joined the civil service to "make a name" for themselves. The power which a government post can bring will be discussed more fully in Chapter 5, however; here it suffices to say that whenever a villager has dealings with the administration, the good offices of even a low-ranking government employee can be invaluable.

Another reason is, of course, the need for cash. Men from households in a wide economic spectrum have or have had salaried employment. Even though the salaries are relatively low (starting at about 70 rupees per month at present), most manage to invest part of their income or to augment it in various ways, and those who have government jobs for many years usually have large amounts of land.

In order to be able to work, however, a man has to make arrangements for his land to be farmed. This is one reason why most government employees are relatively young men, just as migrants to India are. Such men tend either to be still living in joint households or else to have separated so recently that their lands can still be managed by fathers or brothers. If a man has a well-paid post, then it is possible for him to employ a ploughman, but few besides Brahmins do this. Many men have to stop working when there is no one to look after their farms —that is, when their parents become old or die and/or they have no brothers or other close relatives nearby.

Another important factor is proximity to the bazaar. The maximum a man seems prepared to walk is around 45 minutes, so villagers from Duari's three northern wards do not hold government posts (this would also be tied up with literacy, as few inhabitants of these wards have gone to school and so are in a weaker position to compete for jobs).

Literacy, proximity to the bazaar, and ability to arrange for help or paid labour on the farm, therefore, are factors contributing to a man's decision to look for work, and, having once found it, to his continuing in employment. But the factors involved in actually obtaining a post are somewhat different. This is shown by an examination of the men who have held or are holding government posts. On the grounds of literacy and proximity to the bazaar, it might be expected that the majority would be Ramas and Naules, and, indeed, this is the case. But a high proportion of Burtels and Giris who live farther away, in Ward C, have held posts, while almost no Adikaris have done so, although they live in the same ward and are literate.

The fact is that influence of one kind or another is extremely important in obtaining a post (see Caplan 1971), although since the setting up in the mid-1950s of a Civil Service Commission, qualifications count, as well: The Ramas are in the most favoured position of any clan in the village, because the Brahmins among them serve the senior government officials as priests. The Adikaris, on the other hand, have their clients in areas north of Duari, far from the bazaar. Ramas have thus been traditionally associated with the bazaar; many of them spend much of their time there and are intimately acquainted with the bazaar, and hence with district politics.

Once a man obtains a post, he is frequently able to help his kinsmen, as well. For example, one Rama Brahmin now occupies an intermediate post in the land-reform office. Temporary workers are employed seasonally by this office at the relatively high salary of 120 rupees per month. It is no accident that of the twelve Duari men thus far employed in this capacity over the three years since the office opened, eleven have been Ramas, nearly all closely related to him.

A similar situation exists in the small education office, where a Naule has held a post for many years. At the beginning of 1969 two of his kinsmen, both Naules, were also working there. Later in the year, the education officer, an outsider, was given permission by Kathmandu to keep a horse in order to be able to visit schools throughout the district. The Naules put in a word for one of their kinsmen, who was hired as groom.

The importance of kinship and clanship is again demonstrated when we examine employment in the district police. Thirteen Duari men have served in the station in Belaspur Bazaar, while another nine have worked in stations in other areas. When district police headquarters were first opened in the bazaar in 1953, two Duari villagers joined up—a Rama Jaisi, and his wife's brother, an Adikari Chetri. These men now occupy senior posts. Eleven villagers subsequently have joined: two were close relatives of the Chetri; three were closely related to the Jaisi (one, his own brother); another four were also Ramas, although of a different lineage; and one was a Naule, who is married to a Rama girl and lives with her family.[2]

Sometimes, however, villagers will be found working in the same government office not because they are kinsmen or clansmen, but because they belong to rival factions in the village. This is likely to happen if the government department is important in the eyes of the villagers as the court is to Duari people, with their frequent disputes over land. In 1962, the son of the Burtel headman of Duari obtained a job in the court. It was no surprise to anyone when one of the Rama pandits, an opponent of the headman, used his influence to place his own son in the same office. A similar situation obtains in the district council (panchayat) office. Two Ramas have been working there for some time; they joined when it was known as the district development office, before the inception of the panchayat system. With its growth in importance, the Burtel headman decided that it would be useful to have a connection there (and, no doubt, to keep an eye on the Ramas). Eventually, another of his sons succeeded in obtaining a post there.

Apart from the five men working outside the district, there are now twenty

Duari men in salaried employment in the bazaar; three are in the district council office, two in the court, six in the police, two in the land-reform office, one in the bank, one in the high school, one as a cook, and two as teachers based in Belaspur Bazaar but posted to outlying areas of the district. Of these, eleven are Ramas, eight Naules, four Adikaris, and two Burtels; they comprise six Brahmins, fifteen Jaisis, and four Chetris. Even though the Ramas remain the majority, there are proportionately fewer of them working than in the past mainly because some have turned to trade and shopkeeping and politics, instead of salaried employment.

With the exception of the two senior police officers, who have now served fifteen years each, and who intend to continue until they qualify for pensions, no one in the village has worked for most of his adult life; Duari people, on the whole, do not regard government service as a career. The average length of service is around six years, and, of the seventy-three men who have held posts, only twenty-two have exceeded this average. Some men work for a time and then break for several months or years before seeking jobs again. Breaks are usually occasioned by the sickness or death of members of the family and general inability to manage both farming and full-time jobs; furthermore, during the Rana period an employee had little security of tenure, since every appointment was renewable annually (Caplan 1971, p. 276).

One of the concomitants of the relatively short period of service of villagers is that very few are promoted. The majority serve in the lowest ranks, as messengers and menials, although, of the twenty-five men now employed, five occupy relatively senior posts—two in the police, two as clerks in the district council office, and the above-mentioned land-reform officer. Occasionally, promotion is refused by Duari men if it involves transfer to another district. On the whole, however, Duari men serve in the lowest ranks because they have so few qualifications. It is unlikely that this situation will change in the near future because of the low proportion of boys now attending school.

Even high-caste parents have been slow to realise that their caste status and a modicum of literacy no longer suffice as qualifications for a government post. This applies particularly to teaching. In the past, it was easy for Brahmins to obtain teaching posts, and 26 percent of the Brahmins in Duari have worked in this capacity. But at present only two Duari Brahmins are working as teachers, because now they need some training in teaching or else recognised degrees. Not only are few men in the village qualified to teach under the new regulations (four have taken teacher-training courses, and the two pandits are qualified by virtue of their Sanskrit degrees), but fewer are attracted to this sort of work, despite the increase in the number of schools and the demand for teachers. Literate men prefer office jobs in Belaspur Bazaar, which enable them to live at home; teaching frequently means being sent to outlying schools in the district, where they feel isolated among "jungalee" ('primitive') peasants. Others who might in the past have been teachers are turning to shopkeeping, which is more lucrative and which enables them to enjoy the excitement of bazaar life.

Shopkeeping

Together with the growth in the number of government offices in the bazaar, there has come a great expansion in trade and in the number of shops. Just before the revolution there were perhaps a dozen shops in the district capital; now there are close to seventy. The old, established shops are run by Newars, who came originally from Kathmandu as government servants or traders; their descendants are permanent residents in the bazaar. More recently, however, shops have been opened by people living in nearby villages, many of whom commute from their homes daily, just as office workers do. Duari people, like others from surrounding villages, have attempted to profit from the new opportunities.

The first Duari man to establish a business was one of the Rama pandits, who bought land in the bazaar in 1963 and built a house and shop. He rents the house to a government employee, and his son runs the shop, selling cloth, which today has an annual turnover of approximately 30,000 rupees. A second Rama, the brother of the Jaisi police officer, also owned a shop, but it closed down after his death.

In 1964, it was decided to expand the bazaar, into an area to the north of the old bazaar. People who did not possess land in the bazaar were invited to submit their names for plots, and nine men from Duari did so (seven Rama Brahmins and two Rama Jaisis). Only four were successful in the draw: three Brahmins and a Jaisi, all of whom paid the purchase price, which averaged 150 rupees. Since that time, two other Duari men, an Adikari Brahmin and another Rama Jaisi, have bought land in the new area. But by 1969, only two shops had been opened by Duari villagers in the new area of the bazaar, although the four others who own land all say they intend to do so as soon as they can raise the capital.

In addition, in recent years two Rama Jaisis have established shops on the main road to the south, ten miles from the bazaar. However, these are temporary stalls which function only in the winter; and operating in summer also would take the owners away from their fields at the peak agricultural period. In any case, traffic in and out of the district comes to a virtual standstill during those months. A substantial amount of capital[3] is needed to start a successful business, but the profits from a good shop can be high. The bazaar shopkeepers reckon on a clear net profit of 25 percent on most goods they sell. Prices in Belaspur, as in most hill bazaars, are very high. McDougal (1968, p. 41) compared prices at a hill bazaar and a terai bazaar in western Nepal and found that those in the former sometimes exceeded those in the latter by as much as 600 percent. Prices are high not only because of profit margins, but also because of the expenses involved in transporting goods from the terai to the hills. A porter's fee for the seven-day journey, carrying a load of up to eighty pounds, is not less than 50 rupees in the dry, cool season and rises in the hot season to 80 rupees or more.

Because the government offices have injected a large amount of cash into the local economy, people are tending to spend more locally. Although the ideal of each household is still to send one of its members once a year to purchase cloth,

The main street in Belaspur Bazaar winds downhill past shops and government offices.

salt, kerosene, and other necessities in the terai, this appears now to be realised only in a minority of cases. The first reason is that the traditional export, clarified butter, which was the source of cash for purchasing these goods, is not as readily available, and, in any case, dairy products now have a ready market in the bazaar: it is no longer necessary to take them seventy miles in order to sell them, although a few people still do this because they get a better price in the terai.

Another inducement to spend money locally in the bazaar shops is the existence of credit facilities, which are not available in the market towns of the terai. Duari people, like others, tend to buy where they can get credit, and this usually means from Duari shopkeepers or else from those who have some connection with the village. The shop in Belaspur Bazaar which is most patronised by villagers belongs to a Brahmin from a village west of Duari whose son is married to the daughter of one of the Rama pandits; more than half of his credit customers are from Duari. Credit is given most frequently to close relatives, or to those considered most credit-worthy, such as government servants. The latter are naturally the ones who tend to spend the most cash in the bazaar; they buy a wide range of luxury items, such as expensive cigarettes, tea, more and better cloth, soap, and writing materials.

Shopkeeping, then, is considered a desirable occupation: it is highly profitable; it enables a man to be almost permanently in the bazaar with sufficient leisure to gossip and make contacts; and it gives power over others through the granting or withholding of credit. In short, it is the perfect occupation for a politician. It is thus not surprising that the two most wealthy and powerful men in Duari, the Rama pandits, should own shops in the bazaar.

Unskilled Work

Not only high-caste people have benefited directly from the increase in the number of offices and shops in the bazaar. Untouchables are also better off, for their services as labourers are now much in demand for building houses and shops and also for carrying in goods needed by the expanding bazaar economy. Duari village contains the largest number of untouchables in the area; only the bazaar itself has almost as large a population of untouchables, but the majority of these are Cobblers engaged in making shoes and Tailors who do mainly their caste-specific work. On a number of occasions when I took surveys of the unskilled labourers working in the bazaar I found that on any particular day around 90 percent of them were Cobblers from Duari and the remainder were untouchables from the bazaar. Duari Cobblers say that usually it is not difficult to obtain this kind of work in the bazaar, since high-castes from Duari and other villages nearby are unwilling to do such work, but they point out that it is not particularly well paid, at 3 rupees daily, without food (the pay for agricultural work is 2 rupees daily, plus food), and that a job lasts for only a few days at a time. Earning money in the bazaar also means that there is a greater temptation to spend it there—a few cups of tea and a few cigarettes can make a large hole in a day's wages.

The second major source of local cash income for Cobblers is portering, which is better paid than labouring. A porter receives 20 rupees for the two-and-a-half day trip to Lakandra Valley and 50 rupees to the terai, a journey of about a week with a full load. These rates are considerably more during the hot season. Belaspur District does not export anything but butter and a few mandarin oranges, so the main demand is for porters to carry goods in from the south—rice from Lakandra Valley and manufactured goods from the terai. Duari village supplies the surrounding area with porters, and virtually every able-bodied Cobbler does this work at some time during the year, particularly after the rice harvest in Lakandra, when much of the grain to make up local deficits is brought into Belaspur District.

Trading in Rice

Some Cobblers from Duari combine portering with petty trading. They travel in small groups of kinsmen and friends to Lakandra, buy up as much paddy as they can afford, husk it on the spot, carry it back to Belaspur, and sell it at a profit either in the village or in the bazaar to government servants and shopkeepers. Trading in rice in this way has become an important source of cash for many

Cobblers in the village, and furthermore it enables them to make up their own grain deficits more cheaply than if they bought rice locally. Rice in the area of Belaspur Bazaar retails at 40 rupees for a muri of paddy; the price in Lakandra Valley is only 20 rupees. A Duari Cobbler explained his operations as follows:

I buy twenty-five pathis of paddy at a time, which costs me 25 rupees. This I take to the [generator-driven] mill in Lakandra; it costs me another 3 rupees for husking. After this I have eleven pathis of rice. I eat about half a pathi on the journey and bring home one and a half pathis to my family. The remaining nine pathis I sell in Belaspur Bazaar for 4 rupees per pathi. The total profit on the trip is thus 8 rupees in cash, plus the rice that I consume and what I bring home for my family.

Some Cobblers also trade in sugar in this way, although the profits are not as high as they are for rice; sugar is expensive in Lakandra, too, as it is imported from India.

Not only is Lakandra rice important in petty trading; many Cobblers find that they can use the cash they earn locally, either in the village or Belaspur Bazaar, to buy rice in the valley at half the local price. In this way, they can make up their deficits more cheaply, which is why so many of them prefer now to work for cash rather than grain wages. The price of a pathi of paddy is 2 rupees in the Belaspur area; for a day's work, the wages are either one pathi or 2 rupees. If cash is earned, and then taken to be spent in Lakandra, double the amount of paddy can be bought.

Migration to Lakandra

With the eradication of malaria, it has now become possible for hill-dwellers to spend extended periods of time in Lakandra Valley, although most are reluctant to be there for any length of time in the hot season. Six Duari villagers own land in Lakandra; all are Brahmins, and most are Ramas, including the two pandits. One of the latter bought his land around the time of the revolution when prices were still low and, like most other hill families owning land in the valley, engaged Tharus to work it as sharecroppers. Since the eradication of malaria, he has built a house there; and now he and his family spend winters in the valley. None of the other people from Duari who own land in the valley spends any length of time there, but they do visit frequently.

A few of the very poorest untouchable families—Cobblers and Smiths—move to Lakandra for the winter. There they obtain work of all kinds—building, portering, agricultural labour—while at the same time living more cheaply than if they were at home. About a dozen Cobbler and one Smith households moved to Lakandra for the winter of 1968/1969. One family has even acquired a little land there—not, it should be emphasized, choice land which would command a high price, but poor, unused land upon which they have squatted. The head of this household explained how important the valley is for him and his family:

We go to Lakandra every year for four months, the whole family except for my eldest son. I work in the market centre as a house-builder, and my wife and sons also work. Food is cheap there. We earn money and buy rice, some of which we save to bring back to Belaspur with us at the end of the winter. While we are down there, my eldest son comes whenever he can spare time from the farm and he has money, and he buys rice to take back to Belaspur to sell.

As yet, only one or two families from Duari have left the village permanently to live in Lakandra, and these are Cobblers. Hill people from other areas have begun to settle in the valley in large numbers, and the population has increased considerably since the revolution. Lakandra is undoubtedly more attractive to potential emigrants than is the terai, for the former lies at an altitude of 2,000 feet, while the latter is only just above sea-level and its climate is exceptionally trying, particularly in the summer when temperatures of 100°F are not at all uncommon, and in the subsequent monsoon period, when the rainfall is much heavier than in the hills. Moreover, the valley is within easy walking distance of their mountain homes. In the terai, there are government schemes to encourage people to leave the overpopulated hills and develop the land, which is plentiful there. There are added inducements of better communications, transport, hospitals, and schools than are available in the hills, but the factor of climate outweighs all these advantages, and the few villagers who have tried living in the terai have all returned.

It is possible that more families would have left Duari permanently, perhaps to settle in Lakandra, had the pressures on land become acute earlier, as they did in other areas, or had malaria been eradicated earlier. But as it was, the increase of pressure on land in the village coincided with the growth of opportunities to earn cash both locally and in Lakandra and to make up grain deficits by trading. These factors, combined with the strength and importance of kin and village ties, have kept permanent migration from Duari to a minimum.

Summary

The economic situation has been considerably changed by the growth of Belaspur Bazaar and the opening-up of Lakandra Valley. However, the different ways in which members of each caste were able to exploit the new opportunities were already predetermined by such factors as wealth and literacy. The setting-up of the bhasa school in the bazaar increased literacy among the high-castes, particularly those living nearby; at the same time, the fact that the untouchables were debarred from attending meant that they would be confined to unskilled work for the foreseeable future.

The growth of the bazaar since 1951 has accelerated the monetisation of the economy. More money is available locally, and it is increasingly being used to pay for services which were previously paid for in grain. Formerly, cash was in short supply, as is evidenced by the fact that twenty-five years ago it took an unskilled labourer fifty-eight days of work to earn enough cash to buy a muri of paddy, but only twenty days to earn the muri if he were paid in grain. Today, cash is in greater supply, and grain, even among the high-castes, is scarce. Accordingly, cash wages are preferred by both employer and employee. By working for cash, a Cobbler can earn enough money to buy a muri of grain at local prices in twenty days; if he takes his cash and goes to Lakandra Valley, he gets two muris for the same amount of cash, or one muri for ten days' work. It may thus be said that wages have risen more rapidly than prices, although, since the Cobblers have continuously been losing land, their extra cash is spent on making up their greater grain deficits and not on improving their standard of living.

For those in government employment wages have also risen, but most civil servants, who are members of high castes, do not need their salaries to make up grain deficits; they can invest them in buying land and animals; they can also use their cash to enjoy a better standard of living than the Cobblers, particularly in diet, clothing, and housing.

Since more money is earned locally, more tends to be spent locally, too. There is now a large market with a variety of imported goods. Money is spent in the bazaar not only by government servants, but also by villagers, who rely less and less on long trips to the terai for purchase of their annual necessities. Shopkeeping has become a profitable activity, and some people are turning to investment in this field, rather than in land.

What effect has all this had on the relations among the castes in the village, particularly between the Brahmins and the Cobblers? Two major processes may be discerned. The first is that the gulf between them is growing because of an increasing inequality in the distribution of resources.

At the same time, the Cobblers are now far less dependent upon the Brahmins than in the past. The master-ploughman system has declined, and fewer loans are given and certainly fewer lands are mortgaged than formerly. Cobblers still do work for Brahmins, but they are generally paid for it in cash on a daily basis, and they spend this cash not on buying grain from the Brahmins, but on buying it cheaply in Lakandra. Many Cobblers do not work much in the village, but instead labour for wages in the bazaar or in Lakandra. In short, they are much less economically dependent upon the Brahmins than previously, and this has had important repercussions in the political sphere.

NOTES

1. In Nepal this examination is nowadays recognised as the Sanskrit equivalent of a high-school certificate.

2. Marriage is normally virilocal; this was the only instance in the village of uxorilocality.

3. The simplest structure in the bazaar costs about 1,000 rupees to build, and the smallest shop carries a stock worth approximately 500 rupees.

5. Village Politics: Factions

This chapter is concerned with the struggle for power in the village between two rival factions after the revolution of 1951 and, more particularly, after the inception of the panchayat system a decade later. The leaders of the factions recruited their support in the village chiefly along the lines of an already-established dichotomy between groupings based on clan membership. The cleavage between the high-caste clans in Duari has already been mentioned briefly. There are two groupings in the village, the Ramas on the one hand and an alliance of Adikaris, Burtels, and Giris—often supported by the Naules—on the other.

The clans in the latter grouping are linked by residence in one ward, a common era of migration into the village, devotion to the same god, and fictive clanship. The Ramas, on the other hand, arrived later in the village, settled in their own area, and worshipped a different god. This cleavage at times takes the form of intense competition.

However, in the struggle for power, especially for control of the village-council chairmanship, the leaders were obliged to seek support on other bases too: links with outsiders, such as government officials and powerful notables in other villages, were utilised; and the followings of leaders in the two small villages of Magargaon and Toli, which had been incorporated into a single Administrative Village with Duari, had also to be recruited.

The Pre-revolutionary Period

During Rana times, and, indeed, until 1960, Duari village was a separate administrative entity, a revenue unit with its own headman. The latter had responsibility for collecting taxes on lands and houses and for paying them to the senior headman. Headmen might be appointed by senior headmen or directly by the treasury office. To a certain extent, villagers' feelings were taken into account, and a highly unpopular headman would probably be dismissed from office. Both headmen and senior headmen were entitled to a percentage (2.5 percent and 5 percent, respectively) of the taxes they collected, and it is possible that they obtained a little extra, as well. However, they had to account for all the taxes of the units they were assigned, and if some households were unable to pay their taxes for some reason, such as a landslide, then the headman would have to meet those taxes out of his own pocket. Even so, most headmen and senior headmen managed to become wealthy during their periods of office.

Another important advantage of headmanship was the right to three days of free labour annually from each household which paid tax. In 1942, there were 95 such households registered in the village, thus giving the headman 285 man-days of free labour.

The office of headman carried a great deal of prestige and certainly brought a considerable amount of pecuniary and other advantages. The families of the last three—a Rama Brahmin, an Adikari Brahmin, and a Burtel Jaisi—are now among the wealthiest in the village. The Burtel headman, although a Jaisi, owns more village land than anyone else, Brahmins included, most of which was bought while in office. The sons of the now-deceased Adikari headman are also wealthy; they own a large amount of land in the village, and one of them has land in the bazaar and another, land in Lakandra Valley. The Rama former headman, who is still alive, not only owns a great deal of land in the village and in Lakandra, but is the only Duari person with land in the terai.

It is thus likely that the post of headman was sought-after and possible that competition followed the lines of the clan cleavage. But it is not at all clear to what extent or in which contexts this cleavage operated before the revolution of 1951. What is certain is that competition for this post was much more limited than it is for the new post of council chairman. This is because, firstly, the final choice of headman was the prerogative of powers outside the village itself, so that contenders had to depend on links established with government officials or senior headmen and not primarily on support within the village itself. Second, once a headman was appointed, he remained in office until his death or until old age rendered him incapable of performing his duties. The last (Burtel) headman served in that capacity for more than twenty years, and his term of office only ended with the transfer of tax-collection duties to the village council.

Since the inception of the panchayat system, competition has become intense, and those who held power in the old system have sought it in the new. The chief power-seekers in Duari are the former Burtel headman and the close relatives of the former Rama headman, particularly the pandits, one of whom is his son. The Adikaris are no longer active in village politics. As was shown in Chapter 4, very few of them have sought government posts (one avenue to power in the village) in comparison with the many Rama Brahmins who have done so. The Adikaris rationalise the situation by saying, "We are priests, and that is enough. We are simple and good people, not like the Ramas, who are clever and unscrupulous." One explanation may be that the Adikaris' clients are all distributed to the north of the bazaar, and they interact very little with bazaar people. Another may be that they have no highly educated Brahmins among them to act as leaders, as do the Ramas.

The Ramas, on the other hand, have realised more quickly than others the implications of the panchayat system, and this is probably because of their contact with the bazaar, where many of their clients live. And the Burtels, one of whom was the last headman, have been determined not to see their power and influence diminished, particularly as their Jaisi status precludes them from earning a livelihood as priests, unlike many of the Adikaris and Ramas.

However, before going on to discuss the way in which the political cleavage developed in the village after the inception of the panchayat system, the important ties linking the two clan groupings must be examined.

First of all, there are marriage ties. In Duari, as in most of Nepal, there is no rule of village exogamy, such as exists in parts of India. Wives are taken from within the village and from surrounding villages lying within a day's walk of Duari. Most high-caste marriages are extra-village, but 17 percent are intra-village. The latter figure is slightly higher for Brahmins, mainly because there are so few Brahmins in Belaspur District. Marriages, then, take place, subject only to rules of clan exogamy, caste endogamy and hypergamy, and the fictive kinship links between the Burtels, Giris, and Adikaris, which preclude intermarriage between members of these groups. An examination of intra-village marriages does not reveal any particular pattern of clan links, with one exception: the Burtels are nearly all married to Naules, but, since there are many more of the latter than the former, many Naules also are married to Adikaris and Ramas.

There are also the ties of priest and client. The Adikaris serve the Naules and the Ramas as priests, while the Ramas serve the Giris, Burtels and Adikaris. The fact that the Brahmins among the Ramas and the Adikaris have to exchange priestly services with each other is not considered an ideal arrangement, but since no other Brahmins live in the area, there is little choice.

The important point is that there is a web of ties linking the two groupings, and it would thus be impossible for them to break off relations completely, even if they were engaged in an intense struggle for political power, as they were at one period. After the 1951 revolution, these two groupings developed into factions centered around leaders seeking political office in the new panchayat system.

Post-revolutionary Politics: 1951–1961

After the revolution which re-established the power of the monarchy, there was a period of confusion throughout Nepal. Governments were formed and dismissed in fairly rapid succession, and changes in the district administration reflected the power struggles in Kathmandu. The growth of political parties provided new opportunities for ambitious men from the villages to test their strength outside the village arena. Parliamentary elections were held in 1959, bringing a clear victory for the Nepali Congress party. But its term in office was short; in December 1960 the king dissolved parliament and banned political parties.

The turmoil through which Nepal was passing seems to have had little effect on Duari village. A Burtel retained his post as headman, and the majority of villagers seem to have been little interested in party politics. However, there were exceptions to this: the two Rama pandits, then teachers in the bhasa school, played active roles in party politics; one was for a time the district chairman of one of the national political parties.

During this period, the pandits were not particularly involved in village politics; they appear to have been more interested in the political activities being played out in the bazaar. But the two pandits did quarrel with the Burtel headman, and it was this personal antagonism which was to turn the groupings in Duari into factions at a later date. Two disputes, in particular, are worth recounting for the light they shed on later events.

Dispute A. Wife-stealing

Pandit Udey Rama was the priest of Headman Bali Burtel. The former's son "stole" the wife of the latter's son; this would not ordinarily be considered an especially serious offence, but in the circumstances of the priest-client relationship, it was an unforgivable breach of custom and trust. Although the Burtels accepted compensation,[1] they rejected Pandit Udey Rama and took another Rama Brahmin as their priest.

The following year, the headman clashed with both the pandits.

Dispute B. An Attempt to Open a School

Headman Bali Burtel decided to start teaching a small number of children in his own house. He explained that, although there were by that time primary schools both in Magargaon[2] and in the bazaar, both were very far away for the children living near his house. However, most people in this part of the village were Cobblers, and so were most of his pupils.

The Rama Brahmins were furious, and the outcry was led by the pandits. According to Headman Bali: "They frightened the Cobblers so that the latter stopped sending their children to my school after three or four months; they had just about learned to write their own names. The Brahmins thought that if the Cobblers became literate, they would have to plough and carry their own loads, and they didn't like the idea. They said that, as priests, they had to work for their clients and hadn't time to work in their fields as well. So the school just folded up."

Headman Bali Burtel's motives in opening a school largely for Cobblers were never very clear. He claimed he only wanted to help them and referred to the special relationship between the Burtels and the Cobblers.[3]

It is, of course, much plainer why the Brahmins should oppose education for untouchables, although the opposition actually came mainly from the Rama and not the Adikari Brahmins. One reason was the by-then well established enmity between Bali Burtel and the pandits, particularly Udey Rama. Another was the greater orthodoxy in religious and caste matters on the part of the Rama Brahmins, influenced by the pandits.[4] And the pandits, who had spent some time in India, may have realised more than did the less sophisticated Adikaris just what the implications of having literate Cobblers in the village would be for themselves.

The Rama Brahmins were also in a position to threaten the Cobblers. They lent them more money and grain than did the Adikaris and tended to hire more Cobblers as ploughmen and agricultural labourers. And it must be recalled that in 1959 the economic changes described in the last three chapters had not yet really affected the dependence of the Cobblers on the Brahmins. However, the desire to keep Cobblers in their proper place was not the sole reason for opposition by the Ramas, and particularly by the pandits, to the school; they also wanted to strike at their enemy Bali Burtel, and they succeeded in this by threatening the Cobbler pupils and their parents.

The Panchayat System

In 1960 the king dissolved the recently elected parliament, outlawed political parties, and imprisoned many party leaders.[5] A new political and administrative system, based on panchayats was introduced. In Belaspur, the system became operational in 1962. Duari village became part of a larger Administrative Village, which included Magargaon and another high-caste village, Toli. Duari comprises six of the village's nine wards, the Magar village another two, and Toli one.

On each village council, as stated, there are nine members elected from wards and a universally elected chairman and vice-chairman. One member of this council represents the village on the district assembly. The council also appoints a paid secretary. In addition to the village council, there is also a village assembly, which consists of all adults of voting age (twenty-one years or more) resident in the Administrative Village. This assembly meets at least twice yearly to approve the village budgets. The village council is supposed to meet every month.

Those who had been most active politically in the earlier period, particularly the Ramas, now threw themselves into village council politics. The most important reason for this was the nature of the panchayat system, itself: in order to achieve power at a high level (for example, district level), a man must first be elected to office in the Administrative Village. Unlike the party political system, whose smallest organisational units had been large, dispersed constituencies, upward mobility in the panchayat system meant starting at the lowest levels— the ward and village. It was probably only the Ramas who realised the implications of the panchayat system; other villagers were wary of innovations after having seen the fate of political parties and some of their more ardent adherents. In any case, the headman retained his office and his powers, and, even following the establishment of a village council, everything in the village seemed much as before.

Even so, a village council had to be formed; few persons were willing to be members, and no election was held. It seems that some prominent Ramas, primarily the two pandits, and also a wealthy Rama Jaisi who owned a shop in the bazaar (the brother of the police officer) summoned several persons they thought would be suitable, and they became the ward members. Accordingly, the first council consisted of no fewer than six Ramas, one of whom was chairman; two Magars, one of whom was vice-chairman; and a Jaisi from Toli. A Naule was appointed secretary.

Although the Ramas found it easy to dominate the first village council, a struggle did soon develop over the siting of the village council building. As can be seen from Map 2 the most central point in the Administrative Village is Ward C, and, indeed, Headman Bali Burtel proposed that the building should be sited next to an ancient temple there. The Ramas were quick to oppose this, for it would mean that the building would be next door to the headman's house. Instead, they proposed a site on a piece of land in their own Ward A, on the main trail to the bazaar, and there the building was finally erected, even though its situation was inconvenient for the majority of people living in the Administrative Village.

After only two years in office, the Rama chairman resigned because, he said, the post was taking up too much of his time and he wanted to set up a shop in the bazaar, where he had recently bought some land. This man, a rather diffident character, had been guided by the leading Ramas, but he was no longer interested in holding office and has since played no role in village council politics.

A meeting of the village assembly was called, and Ganga Rama, brother of the police officer, was confirmed as chairman. It may seem surprising that the headman did not oppose the Rama candidature, but it seems likely that even at that stage (1963), the panchayat system was still having very little effect on the village. This was soon to change.

In 1964, the Land Reform Act, whose economic effects have been discussed, was passed. Headmen and senior headmen were deprived of their rights to collect tax and enjoy free labour from the households in their revenue units. The former powers were given to the village councils, while the latter were abolished. Village councils were also invested with other powers and duties: They were allowed to fine people for minor offenses; they issued letters of recommendation to those wanting government posts; they dealth with most matters pertaining to land reform, such as the completion of the census and a registration of debts and loans; they were also provided with large sums of money for development purposes. These changes prompted many former headmen and senior headmen to enter the arena of panchayat politics and to seek office in the new system.

The 1966 Election

In 1966, Ganga Rama's term as council chairman came to an end, and for the first time an election was held. The incumbent Ganga Rama was defeated by the former headman Bali Burtel; another candidate, the former headman of Toli village, ran a poor third.

What were the bases on which these men recruited support? Within Duari village the alignments were fairly clear, and they were based on high-caste clan affiliation. The core of Bali Burtel's support came from members of his own clan and from Adikaris and Giris, with whom they have fictive kinship ties. The Ramas provided the core of Ganga Rama's backing, led by the pandits. Most of the Naules supported Bali Burtel, largely because of affinal ties. In terms of voters, these two groupings were about equal (see Table 3).

However, the introduction of universal suffrage meant that the untouchables also had become politically important, and in Duari they constitute half the population. They do not like the Ramas and, as has been mentioned, blame them for the loss of their lands. They also maintain there is a special link between the Burtel-led grouping and the Cobblers, who had originally "shown" them their land. Accordingly, they all voted for Bali Burtel.[6]

A Factional Leader as Chairman

During Bali Burtel's term as village council chairman, the factional cleavage widened, with the pandits using all their resources of wealth, government contacts, and Rama clan backing to oppose the chairman, while the latter, in turn, sought to consolidate his position, particularly by using the powerful weapon of his office. One way in which Bali Burtel did this was by cracking the Rama hegemony on the village council. By the end of his term of office, only two Ramas remained as council members, whereas six had been members when the council was originally set up. While Bali Burtel was chairman a second Cobbler, a Naule, and an Adikari replaced Ramas on the council.[7]

However, the council's representative to the District Assembly remained a Rama, the brother of Pandit Kanak Rama, and there is little doubt that the pandits made greater efforts to keep him in office than they did ordinary council members. This is because it was in their interest to have someone close to them with a position in political circles beyond the village level. The village representative attends the district assembly and has a vote in elections for the district council. The pandits, themselves, while playing a vital role in Duari politics, are also actively interested in politics at the district level. Bali Burtel, on the other hand, was only interested in power within the village, and, indeed, his lack of political or administrative contacts in the bazaar probably contributed to his eventual loss of office in Duari.

The fact remains, however, that while he holds office the chairman is a powerful man. Two disputes which occurred during Bali Burtel's term illustrate how the power of the chairmanship itself and the backing of the village council place a very important weapon in the hands of a factional leader.

Dispute C. The Thakuri's Land

Formerly, a Thakuri family was living in Duari. The household consisted of a man and wife and their only son, Narayan. The latter in around 1959 migrated to India, and his parents later heard that he had become an ascetic *(saddhu)* in a temple there. His father went around the village borrowing money to raise the fare to India, to persuade his son to return home. He borrowed principally from his nearest neighbour, Pandit Kanak Rama, to whom he mortgaged two plots of rice land.

The old man did find his son, but to his grief, the boy refused to speak to him, as he had taken a vow of silence. On his return to Duari, the father died, and his wife outlived him by only a few days. The family had no other relatives living in Duari, although the old man's married sister was in a neighbouring village. The child of this marriage took upon himself the responsibility for the funeral rites and carried out the mourning as if for his own parents. The priest was Pandit Kanak Rama, and he also contributed some of the funeral expenses.

The property left consisted of movable assets, which were taken by the sister's son who had arranged the funeral rites, some rice land, and a plot of dry land. The rice land was being cultivated by Pandit Kanak Rama in return for the money he had lent the old man; the dry land was taken by the sister's son, who put it up for sale. The pandit protested, saying that Narayan (the ascetic) was still alive and might one day return to claim his inheritance. The pandit claimed that he had written to Narayan in India, telling him of the death of his parents and of his own help in the funeral rites.

The pandit received a letter in reply, asking him to look after the land until Narayan should return some time in the future. The pandit's enemies, particularly the council chairman, Bali Burtel, claimed that the letter was a forgery, which the pandit had written himself. Similar letters were received by the former senior headman and the governor of the district; all of these, council chairman Bali Burtel contended were forgeries and a trick of the pandit's to get the land for himself. The chairman even argued that the pandit had no right to use the rice land because the old man had told him a few days before his death that he had paid off the loan to the pandit and had redeemed the land.

Chairman Bali Burtel also maintained that Pandit Kanak Rama had offered him a bribe to register the dry land in his—the pandit's—name. He claimed to have refused to do this and referred the matter to the district council. There it was decided that the land should be administered by the village council until such time as Narayan returned from India. Accordingly, bids for the tenancy of the land were invited.

The highest bid was made by a Cobbler, Kalo, who said that he would pay 8½ muris of grain annually as rent to the council. He became the tenant in 1965, after selling the little land he owned to Bali Burtel and another Cobbler. He managed to pay the rent for the first year, but thereafter claimed that the total yield of the land was less than 8½ muris and that it was therefore impossible for him to pay anything.

Kalo maintained that he had been misled by Pandit Kanak Rama, for whom his son worked as ploughman. It was he who had persuaded Kalo to apply for the tenancy. Kalo explained: "When this land came up, the Pandit called me and gave me a cigarette and told me that this was a golden opportunity which should not be missed. He advised me to bid for the land for a rental of three muris of grain. He also promised me unlimited help in cultivating the land—that he would lend me seeds and bullocks. On the day of the auction, the pandit took me by the arm, and we went there together. When the bidding got higher than 3 muris, I asked the pandit why he himself didn't bid, as he is a rich man and the land adjoins his, but he told me to keep on bidding. But when I became the tenant, he started making life difficult for me. He did not give me any of the help he had promised; on the contrary, he allowed his cattle to graze on my land and sent his family to pick oranges off my trees. He also refused to give my son his grain dues [for working as ploughman], so he refused to work for the pandit any more. Then the pandit went to the Land-Reform office to complain that my son still owed him money and to get the land we rented registered in his own name."

The pandit had a different version, maintaining that the owner of the land, Narayan, had given the land to him in trust and, furthermore, that he was owed money by the estate of Narayan's father for performing the funeral rites. He also argued that the land should produce at least sixteen muris of grain annually, but that Kalo and his family had been neglectful in spending every winter in Lakandra and letting the rented land go to ruin.

The dispute over who had the right to use the land continued. Kalo petitioned the court, the land-reform office, and the district council, not to mention a variety of senior government officials who happened to visit the district, requesting that the rent be reduced or that he be excused past payment. As an illiterate and poor Cobbler, Kalo was in no position to gain the ear of even the most minor government official, but all his petitions were written for him by Chairman Bali Burtel, for whom another of his sons worked as ploughman. While he was chairman, Bali Burtel was able to see that Kalo was not turned off the land for failure to pay the rent to the village council. But the pandit, being an educated man with influence in the bazaar, could see to it that no decision was made which would reduce the rent or excuse the rent already owed by the Cobbler. The pandit hoped that eventually Kalo would be evicted and that he would be given the use of the land himself; but as long as Bali Burtel was council chairman, he was not able to do this.

The situation was quite clear to the majority of villagers, and they criticised Pandit Kanak Rama, pointing out that he was already the richest man in the village, that he had more than enough land, and that to make such a fuss over the 70 rupees he claimed he was owed for the funeral rites was ridiculous. But most expected that he would eventually get the land if Bali Burtel ceased to be chairman, because of his contacts in the bazaar, particularly with the younger brother of Pandit Udey Rama, an official in the land-reform office.

At the end of my fieldwork, the case had not been decided, although Kalo was still having petitions written for him by Bali Burtel. However, the latter was no longer chairman, and consequently the Cobbler had been served with several eviction notices by the village council.

Dispute D.   Settling on Grazing Land

Pandit Kanak Rama is the eldest of five brothers, Their father died before any of them had separated from the joint household. When the brothers did split up, the property division was made by the pandit, as the eldest. One of the younger brothers told me that he thought that the pandit had made the allocation of land and clients (jajmans) to his own advantage and to the detriment of his younger brothers. In fact, the pandit's four brothers are relatively poor Brahmins, and none of them owns sufficient land to cover his own needs, although they do, of course, receive grain from their clients. Their relative poverty is highlighted by the wealth of their eldest brother.

In 1967, three of the brothers decided that they would have to acquire more land. Encouraged by the pandit, they took over an area of land used by the villagers for grazing cattle, and began to cultivate and build houses there.

To some extent, a precedent existed: only a few years before, a group of ascetic women, who had been settled for some time in the village, had been given a piece of grazing land by the village council on which to build a temple and a retreat *(kuti)* for themselves. The idea of giving them this land had come from the then-chairman Ganga Rama, supported by Pandit Kanak Rama, on whose land they had previously been living.

However, when the pandit's brothers took over a large area of land next to that occupied by the ascetics, there was an outcry, led by Chairman Bali Burtel. He said that the matter had never been put before the village council and that if it had been, it would never have been passed, because these were Brahmins who were far from being the poorest in the village. Furthermore, it would establish a precedent, which might lead to the loss of all the remaining grazing lands. He also pointed out that the pandit was very wealthy and accused him of encouraging his brothers to take over the grazing land in order to avoid having to give them their fair share of the inheritance.

Chairman Bali Burtel sent a complaint to the district council, and the matter also went before the court, the treasury (which registers land), and the land-reform office. At first, no action was taken, and the pandit urged his brothers to complete the building of their houses as quickly as possible. The brothers received a warning from the police that their land might be taken from them and their houses demolished, and the court ruled that they had no right to the land. However, when the police did come to the village, the houses were completed, and the police maintained that the Brahmins had established a *de facto* right; the police went away without doing anything.

By 1969, the land was still not registered in the treasury, but the brothers were paying compulsory savings on its produce, which meant that they had been given *de facto* recognition by the land-reform office.

These disputes demonstrate how leaders of factions operate. In neither case were Bali Burtel and Pandit Kanak Rama competing directly, but although they claimed only to be supporting those directly involved, in effect, they were the main protagonists. In Dispute C, the pandit claimed that he was protecting the rights of Narayan in the latter's absence, while Bali Burtel claimed to be helping a poor Cobbler. In Dispute D, Bali Burtel maintained that he was on the side of the village, protecting scarce common lands against encroachment, while the pandit said that he was helping his brothers to exercise their rights as citizens to take up and cultivate unused land.

Both sides used all means available for conducting their disputes—Bali Burtel, his power and influence as council chairman, and the pandit, his connections with government officials in the bazaar. It is no accident that in Dispute D, of the four government offices concerned, the three in which Ramas worked (district council, land reform, and police) did not take direct action against the pandit's brothers; the fourth, the treasury, which refused to register the land in the brothers' names, contained no Ramas.

The status and connections of the pandit should have enabled him to have the upper hand in both disputes, were it not for the important fact that Bali Burtel was the village council chairman, which gave him direct access to senior government officials. Largely because of these disputes, both pandits realised that it was in their interests to control the village council themselves. They decided to challenge Bali Burtel's chairmanship, and to do so as quickly as possible, rather than waiting until the latter's term had expired.

The Attempt to Expel the Chairman

The pandits and various other Ramas drew up a complaint, which they circulated around the village. This document, a proposal of "no confidence" to be put before the village assembly, accused council chairman Bali Burtel of corruption, embezzlement of funds, falsifying land records, and more. The text was as follows:

The Chairman of this Village Council is abusing his office. For example, he has embezzled the aid given by the District Council for building irrigation channels and for completing the construction of the Village Council building. He cannot give a correct account of the income and expenditure of the compulsory savings scheme, which is collected in the form of grain. We have complained about this to the District Office, and he has been instructed to redistribute this grain to the villagers, but so far he has not done so. Furthermore, he has been selling off valuable trees. He has also been charging each household two rupees for completing the land reform forms. On these forms he has put down land in the names of children, he has tried to register one person's land in the name of someone else. In addition, he has tried to cause fighting between people, and has charged unnecessary taxes. He has also hidden the copy of the minutes of the last Village Council meeting and pretended that he lost them. Since he became Chairman, he has not called a single Council meeting until now. He sent letters to all the ward representatives on the Council, threatening to implicate them all in the matter of the embezzled money, and telling them that they must back him in whatever he says [to the authorities]. All the documents concerned with his tricks are now with the District Council office and we hope that everything will soon be cleared up. Since this Chairman has used public property for himself, and has tried to weaken the panchayat system, we submit this proposal of no confidence in him. At the next Village Assembly when this document has been approved, arrangements should be made for electing a more suitable Chairman.

There then followed a total of 159 signatures; of these, a quarter were illegible, another quarter were those of Ramas, a quarter were of untouchables, and the remainder were Naules and Adikaris. It is hardly surprising that a substantial proportion of the signatories were Ramas and that no Burtel or Giri signatures appeared. What may require more explanation is why any Adikaris, traditionally supporters and "brothers" of the Burtels, should have signed, even though only a few of them did so, and also why more than a third of the Naules in the village also signed. Even more surprising is the large number of untouchables who signed.

Three major explanations were given by the villagers. The illiterates, mainly Cobblers, claimed that they had been misled about the contents of the petition. One Cobbler told me, "They [some Ramas] came in the night and told us that the petition was something to do with land reform, and so we signed it [by applying thumbprints]. We were under the impression that it was an appeal for us to get back some of our lands we had lost by mortgaging. Three days later, everyone knew the contents of the petition, and I went to the pandits and told them to cross off my name, and that I, like all the Cobblers, supported Bali Burtel."

Some literate persons claimed that they, too, had been duped; they said that the petition had been changed after they had signed it. One man told me that the original document accused Bali Burtel of such misdeeds as allowing trees to be cut down and that the pandits had added other charges of a more serious nature after the signatures had been collected.

The Adikaris, only a few of whom had signed the petition, had done so for different reasons. The compulsory grain savings for Ward C, the chairman's own ward, had been collected by the ward representative, an Adikari Brahmin, who stored them in his brother's house. When the pandits began to accuse Bali Burtel of using the grain savings for himself, an examination revealed that, in fact, the savings did appear to be short. The chairman, however, contended that they had been "eaten" by the ward representative and accused the Adikari brothers of misappropriating 80 rupees' worth of grain. The Adikaris were furious and said that Bali Burtel was merely trying to cover up his own misdeeds; when the petition was prepared, the brothers and their immediate relatives naturally signed.

As a result of this petition being presented at the district council office and in view of a number of earlier complaints about the compulsory grain savings, the chairman was suspended from office. After some time, a village assembly was called by the Magar vice-chairman, who also asked some notables from surrounding villages to attend, including the former senior headman of the area. The matter was debated at length, and the chairman, Bali Burtel, emerged victorious. This account of the meeting was given by one of the notables from another village:

> We asked the Assembly if Bali Burtel had done anything wrong, and we said that if he had taken money, then they ought to go ahead and punish him; but if he had not, then we wanted to know what the complaint was about. The Cobblers said that he had done nothing wrong and had given them no problems, so we asked why they had signed the document. They replied that they had been told that it concerned other matters; they hadn't known the real contents of the paper.
>
> So the Ramas were found out, and we asked them if this was the kind of thing they did —writing false charges, and making illiterate people sign such documents. We told them they deserved to be beaten, but they went away. They had even put the names of dead women on that document! Those Ramas just wanted to drive Bali Burtel out and get his post for themselves.

The man who gave me this account is an affine of Bali Burtel and supported him at the meeting, so his version is hardly unbiased. It may be compared with accounts of the assembly given by the pandits:

> PANDIT UDEY RAMA: We made a complaint of dishonesty against Bali Burtel because when he was chairman he made a mess of everything. Development projects were not finished, and the district council refused to give more money until they were. He used the development money himself, as well as tax money, and he didn't take the proper steps to ensure that Kalo Cobbler paid the rent for Narayan's land. Why was the petition defeated in the Assembly? He [Bali Burtel] sent his son in the night to the houses of various Cobblers and persuaded them to say that they had not signed the paper at all, and to support Bali Burtel in the assembly. So all the Cobblers came to the assembly, men, women, and children, and voted for Bali Burtel. They were organised for him and by him.

> PANDIT KANAK RAMA: Why wasn't he dismissed, when so many people had signed the document? Because notables came from other villages, such as the senior headman, and supported him. They said "You fools, this old man has served you so long—do you want to complain about him?" Because these people [the senior headman and other notables] had given them grain and loans, the Cobblers were frightened into saying that they hadn't signed the document and didn't know anything about it. They said no, the complaints against him were untrue, and clapped their hands [to show support for Bali Burtel]. They were made to say that they had thought they were signing about another topic. So Bali Burtel was not dismissed.

What does emerge from these accounts is the support Bali Burtel received from the Cobblers, particularly in terms of numbers, and from outside notables, particularly the former senior headman, who had by then become an influential politician in the bazaar. Bali Burtel had served as headman under the latter for many years and thus might have expected his support, but there was another and more important reason—namely, a bitter quarrel between the former senior headman and Pandit Udey Rama.

Dispute E.   Priest and Client Disagree

Before 1954, Pandit Udey Rama had been serving as the senior headman's priest. The senior headman had asked the pandit to become his priest because he thought that a man of his stature ought to use a superior Brahmin, a pandit, and not just an ordinary priest. Obviously, since the senior headman was one of the richest and most important men in the district, the pandit agreed to serve him.

The pandit told me how the quarrel came about: "The senior headman's former priest [who lived in another village] put pressure on him to change back, but the senior headman refused. When his wife died in 1954, I officiated at the funeral rites, and received about 3,000 rupees in gold, cattle, and clothing. Seven years later, the senior headman himself died, and in spite of the protests of the former priest, I again performed the ceremonies and I received even more this time. He was succeeded by his son, and the new senior headman asked me to continue being the family priest. I performed the wedding ceremonies for one son of the new senior headman, and for his brothers' sons. However, when the time came for the second son of the senior headman to be married, I had an important rite[8] elsewhere, so I offered to send my son or my brother to officiate at the wedding in my stead. However, the senior headman allowed his old priest to perform the ceremony. A similar thing happened when the senior headman's brother's son was to be married, and, since then, I have not been his priest."

Opinions as to the exact reason for the open breach between the pandit and the senior headman are contradictory. Some claim that it was because the pandit is known to drink alcohol, which is forbidden to high Hindus. Others say that he had a Chetri mistress. Yet others blame the pandit's sons, two of whom had run off with other men's wives.[9]

The senior headman is said to have felt that such behaviour on the part of his priest's family reflected on his own prestige. Whatever the truth of the matter, the fact is that by the mid-1960s, the senior headman and the pandit were enemies, and the former accordingly backed Bali Burtel in his fight against the pandits.

The senior headman did not, of course, attack the pandits in terms of the previous dispute when he supported the chairman in the village assembly. Instead, he brought up a dispute which the pandits had had with the old Kathmandu Pandit who had founded the bhasa school in the bazaar. It was claimed that the pandits had tried to get rid of the old teacher in order to gain control of the bhasa school themselves; this had led to a court case in which they had been accused of forgery. So the senior headman reminded his audience that the pandits had once been convicted of forgery. If they could behave in this way once, then it was likely that they could do so again, he implied. A Cobbler told me,

"This case was brought up as an example of the wickedness of these people; everyone knew that they were cheaters and liars."

Finally, a vote was taken in the assembly; only eleven persons voted for the motion against Bali Burtel. The minutes of the assembly state merely that "item three on the agenda was a discussion about the proposal of no confidence in the chairman, but it was rejected by all present." Those few who did vote against Bali Burtel were Ramas, particularly the core of the pandits' faction.

After the assembly Bali Burtel was reinstated as council chairman. But the pandits had succeeded in their objectives to some extent. Not only had Bali Burtel been suspended from office for several months, but, as a direct result of the petition, he had quarrelled with the Adikaris. Furthermore, the district council office had recommended that, in future, grain savings and all money handled by the village council should be dealt with by the secretary appointed by the council, rather than by the chairman.

Summary

Much of this chapter has taken the form of an extended case history: Bali Burtel's rise to office and the attempts of the pandits to unseat him. In the struggle for control of the village council, these men became leaders of what I have termed factions. This use of the term may be questioned, and, indeed, some writers who have referred to lineages as factions (for example, Lewis 1954) have been criticised (see Nicholas 1965); however, I will briefly try to justify this usage.

According to Nicholas, who follows Firth (1957), a faction is a political conflict group, which is non-corporate and whose members are recruited by a leader on diverse principles. It is, perhaps, the latter part of the definition which needs discussion with reference to Duari's groupings.

First, although in terms of descent the clans are structural groupings, they are not opposed politically on the basis of segmentary principles. Second, although faction leaders here recruit support mainly on the basis of real or fictive kinship and clanship ties, support is given to them on a personal basis; it is not given because the faction leaders hold any positions of formal authority within the groupings. As a result, direct relations between the leader and his individual supporters are more important than relations among the supporters, themselves. This is clearly shown by the result of the personal quarrel between Bali Burtel and some of the Adikaris, which led the latter to sign the petition against the chairman.

The structure of factions should also be examined. Each faction consists of a leader (or leaders, in the case of the Ramas), plus a core (sometimes called a clique) of ardent supporters, usually close kinsmen: Bali Burtel's most active supporters are his adult sons, while those of the pandits are members of their own lineage. In addition, there are ordinary members, whose role is usually passive; in Duari, the ordinary members consist of the remaining Rama lineages, who support the pandits, and the Adikaris, Giris, and Naules, who support Bali Burtel.

Two categories of links used for the recruitment of support may be distinguished, which I term active and reactive. The former category is composed, in this instance, largely of kinship/clanship ties within the village; the core and ordinary members of a faction are recruited in this way. But reactive links can be vital, particularly in a crisis. By reactive links I mean support given to a factional leader (A) by a person (C), who is not normally A's supporter, but who is anxious to thwart A's opponent (B); or where factional leader A is supported by C simply because C's opponent (D) supports A's rival B.

Several examples of reactive links have been given in this chapter. The people of Magargaon are divided into two factions, so that, when one faction gives its electoral support to Bali Burtel, the other supports the Ramas, not because of any links with the latter, but simply to oppose their own enemies. Another instance is that of the senior headman who came to Bali Burtel's defence at the village assembly principally because of his quarrel with one of the pandits, not because he was normally a member of Bali Burtel's faction.

Almost any dispute in the village is "fed" into the factional conflict. If a leader of one faction becomes involved in a dispute with another person, the leader of the other faction immediately steps in to defend the latter, and the leaders themselves become the chief protagonists. This is likely to happen even when no leader is involved initially.

Although the factions are concerned with village politics, disputes in which they become involved are rarely confined to the village. Most are referred by the leaders to government offices, in the hope that greater authority can be enlisted in support of the cause. This is not surprising in view of the absence of any mechanism for settling disputes between important leaders within the village. This, of course, gives the leaders a chance to call on other links—the pandits use their informal ties with kinsmen or clients who are government officers, while Bali Burtel, at least during his chairmanship, used the official channels of the panchayat system. Frequently, disputes which are treated in this way are phrased by the protagonists in terms of government policy—preservation of the forests, mismanagement of development funds, blocking the progress of the village, and so on—in order to cater to a more powerful symbolism than the petty quarrels which form the substance of factional opposition.

NOTES

1. If a married woman runs off with another man, the latter has to pay compensation (*jarikal*) to the first husband; she is then legally considered his wife.

2. This was not to receive government aid or recognition for another two years, and Magargaon and Duari were still separate administrative entities.

3. For the myth which validates this relationship and further discussion, see Chapter 6.

4. See Chapter 6.

5. For a good account of events from 1950 to 1960, see Joshi and Rose 1966.

6. Had the voting been confined to Duari village, Bali Burtel's majority would have been much larger than it was. However, Magargaon, comprising two wards, is split into two factions, which will support opposing candidates on an issue such as this.

The third candidate, from Toli, could use no other ties than his own village ones. Since his is a small village comprising only one ward, it is not surprising that he received few votes. It is possible that, had he not stood for election, the outcome would have been different, since the voting for Bali Burtel and Ganga Rama was close.

7. It is not difficult for the chairman to replace some council members with people of his own choosing. A proportion of council seats become vacant every two years, and so far no elections for these posts have been held. New ward representatives tend to appear who have usually been appointed by the chairman. Furthermore, even when a member's term has not expired, an excuse can be found to get rid of him. For instance, to expel the brother of Pandit Udey Rama, the chairman invoked a rule that council members could lose their seats if they failed to attend three consecutive meetings.

8. The rite was *sapta,* which can only be performed by a pandit; it would earn even more for him than a rich man's wedding.

9. One was the wife of Bali Burtel's son (see Dispute A, p. *61*).

6. Village Politics:
The Growth of Caste Conflict

The incident concerning the petition—Bali Burtel's suspension from the chairmanship of the village council and his subsequent reinstatement after the village assembly—marked a watershed in village politics. Up to that time, the factional leaders had used traditional links, principally those of clanship and fictive-clanship, in seeking support. But, as both leaders discovered, these ties were not sufficient to win elections and, thus, control of the council. Not only does neither factional leader command an electoral majority in Duari, since the two clan groupings are approximately of equal size, but, in addition, one-third of the voters, who live in the villages of Toli and Magargaon, do not have links of clanship with either leader. Finally, the untouchables also have votes and they comprise half of Duari's population. In short, it has become necessary for the factional leaders to seek support through different types of links than the ones previously used.

The 1969 Election

Two candidates presented themselves for election as chairman in 1969, Bali Burtel, the incumbent, and a young former civil servant, Daya Rama, who, it was generally agreed, had been put up by the Rama pandits. Daya Rama, however, does not belong to the pandits' lineage, and he lives in Ward F, away from the main Rama settlement area; for this reason, he is not too closely identified with the pandits.

It may be asked why the pandits had not either put forward a member of their own lineage as candidate or why one of them had not stood, himself. The chief reason given by the villagers was the personal unpopularity of the members of the pandits' lineage, most of whom are Brahmins and money-lenders. Obviously, the same sort of reason can be given for the reluctance of the pandits to put themselves forward, but there were other reasons, as some villagers recognised clearly. One man said, "Those Brahmins [the pandits] don't stand, themselves; they are too clever. They use others, and hold the real power in their own hands. Daya Rama is always going to ask them for advice."

The pandits themselves claimed that they would not stand in an election because, as one of them pointed out, such a person has to mix with all kinds of people, and this would be impossible for men of their status. This may indeed have been an important factor. The pandits saw the holding of office and their high ritual status, which brought them such high incomes, as incompatible.

The leaders of the Rama faction and their core of supporters canvassed vigorously for Daya Rama in their own ward and in the Naule ward (Ward B). Daya Rama, himself, and other Ramas living in Ward F canvassed support there and also in Magargaon. Daya Rama's house lies very close to this village, and his children attend the Magar school, so he probably was able to win votes in this area on personal grounds.

Bali Burtel, on the other hand, did not organise a group of supporters to do any canvassing. One of his sons said, "My father worked for this village for over thirty years—everyone knows what kind of person he is, so why should he solicit votes?" But there seems little doubt that the efforts of Daya Rama and his fellow clansmen had a powerful effect. People spoke admiringly of Daya Rama's ability as a speaker, and his knowledge of "modern things"; they thought that he would be able "to stand up to government officials".

Each side alleged that the other was using unfair methods to win support. Bali Burtel, said the Ramas, had promised the untouchables a feast of buffalo (meat) if he won, while Bali Burtel said that the Ramas had done the same.

Approximately 57 percent of those eligible to vote did so, and Bali Burtel was defeated by a narrow majority of nineteen votes. Although the ballot had been secret, it was generally agreed that voting patterns had been fairly clear-cut. Bali Burtel had the support of virtually all the untouchables, some of the Naules— particularly those affinally connected to him—and one of the Magar factions; he also had the votes of the Giris and his own Burtel clansmen. Daya Rama was supported by all his clansmen, one of the Magar factions, most of the Toli villagers,[1] some Naules, and some Adikaris. Most villagers said that Bali Burtel had received the untouchables' votes and Daya Rama those of the high-castes. This is an oversimplification, but it does indicate the fact that the Ramas had managed to split the opposing alliance of non-Rama high-caste clans, which most villagers saw as a trend toward conflict between high-castes and untouchables.

Four major reasons are given by villagers for Bali Burtel's defeat. The first two are concerned with the way the election was conducted. The polling booth was near the village council building, which is situated just above the Rama ward (Ward A). For the people in Wards D, E, and F, and in the two villages north of Duari, this was a long way to come, and fewer of them than Ramas were seen to vote. In addition, the election was held during the height of the maize-planting season, and many did not vote because they were busy in the fields. A factor which militated particularly against the untouchables was that many of them were making their last portering or trading trips before the monsoon, and a large proportion of them was not in the village at the time of the election. Finally, the fact that each ward was allotted a separate time of day to vote did not help; time is a fairly meaningless concept to most people in the village—meetings can be called for 10:00 A.M. and start at 2:00 or 3:00 P.M. Some people might just have become tired of waiting for their turn to vote and left.

Second, some people appear to have been very confused about what they were free to do and what the government was telling them to do. The polling officer was from the land-reform office,[2] and, his job was merely to ensure that the election was properly conducted. But Pandit Udey Rama's younger brother, who worked in the same office, was also standing near the polling booth canvassing support for Daya Rama. He was not an election official; he had merely taken time off in order to help his candidate. But many people thought he was the polling officer and that he was telling them to vote for Daya Rama, meaning that Daya Rama was the government-backed candidate.

The third reason given for Bali Burtel's defeat may be termed personal factors. Even his most ardent supporters admit that he is now old and often sick. The image he presents is not convincing, some people say. Just before the election, he had lost a lot of land in another village, in a court case which everyone had judged hopeless. Several people remarked, "He lost his dignity by contesting that case, and his popularity went too". It is also generally felt that Bali Burtel "does not understand the panchayat system" and does not know how to deal with government officials. With the greater intrusion by the government into village affairs, it is thought that the council chairman ought to be someone dynamic, who will get as much as possible for the village.

It is generally agreed that, while in office, Bali Burtel had shown none of these qualities. Many have been disappointed by his performance, and they particularly blame him for the unsatisfactory results of land reform. At the time of the implementation of land reform in the village, Bali Burtel had been responsible for filling out the forms disclosing ownership of lands and information about credit and debt. Those who failed to recover lands they had lost in the past blame him, saying, "he would tell people they were going to get their lands back, even when this was clearly impossible".

Bali Burtel is also blamed for the fact that the compulsory grain-saving scheme was not a success. It is, of course, possible that he did misappropriate some of the grain, as his enemies alleged. It is also likely that some of it found its way into the stores of the ward representatives. Similarly, with money for development projects given by the district council—in several instances, jobs, such as the building of an irrigation channel, were contracted out to villagers who spent the money on their own more pressing needs and failed to complete the project.

Usually, the district council only gives half the money needed for a project; the rest is supposed to be made up by villagers in cash contributions and voluntary labour. Very little of this "self-help" is ever forthcoming, so development money tends to melt away, and the chairman is invariably blamed for failing to "develop the village".

In general, however, it seems likely that the amount of paper work and balancing of books required by the panchayat system is far beyond the capabilities of men like Bali Burtel. But most people do not distinguish the difficuties inherent in the chairman's role from the incumbent's personal weaknesses. Bali Burtel was blamed for many frustrations, and it was generally said that the village "needed a new leader".

Analysis of the Election

These are all important reasons for the result of the election, but the factor of greatest interest is the way in which it has come to be seen as a conflict between high and low castes. Bali Burtel, himself, says that "Daya Rama was the Brahmins' candidate" and that the untouchables had wanted him to be their candidate. One high-caste man said disgustedly, "Bali Burtel made himself the untouchables' slave".

Why do the untouchables support the Burtels so strongly? Some of the reasons have already been given, such as their dislike of the Ramas because they blame them for the loss of their lands. In many ways this attitude is somewhat illogical, for the Burtels and the Adikaris also used to lend money, and the latter also occasionally gave mortgages. But the stereotype remains—the Ramas are unscrupulous and give loans because they are avaricious, whereas the Adikaris and Burtels "give loans to help us, and if they take our lands it is by agreement", as one Cobbler put it. Others say that the Adikaris, Burtels, and Giris always pay fair wages and are helpful with small loans and gifts to those who work for them. The Ramas are blamed for most of the Cobblers' present disabilities, and particularly for the denial of education to the untouchables.

The good relations between the Cobblers and the Burtels, in particular, are explained by the following legend, which is known to many villagers:

Legend D.   How the Burtels Helped the Cobblers

In the time of the Belaspur king, a slave girl was turned out of the palace for failing to do her work properly. She went down the hillside to Duari village, and she met a Cobbler who was living there. They lived together and had twelve sons. Later she left this man and went to live with a Smith, by whom she had one son.

Much later, one of the descendants of the Belaspur king, a Thakuri, now living in a neighbouring village, claimed that all the Cobblers and Smiths in Duari were his slaves because they were descended from the Belaspur king's slave girl. The matter was taken to a local court, and the Cobblers were defended by a Burtel, Bali Burtel's Brahmin ancestor, who argued that they were freeborn. After several hearings and appeals, the Cobblers and Smiths were allowed their freedom.

When this Burtel man died, his widow decided to commit *suti*.[3] She called together all her family and all the Cobblers and Smiths, and spoke her last words. She told the Cobblers that just as they had trusted her husband, so they should trust his sons and his sons' sons. And she told her family that they should always protect the untouchables in the village. Then she committed suti, and the words of this virtuous woman are remembered to this day by the Cobblers, and Smiths, and the Burtels.

A family of untouchables stands by its house in Duari. Untouchables here have only recently begun to be conscious of themselves as a group with political importance.

The Cobblers and Bali Burtel need each other. The Cobblers have no leader of their own, for a number of reasons. For one thing, almost all of them are illiterate. Another is that only very recently have they begun to see themselves as a group in opposition to the high castes. But it is very difficult for them to organise, not only because of lack of education, but also because many of them are highly mobile, spending much of their time away in Lakandra Valley or India. It also seems likely that the few untouchables who might have the ability to become leaders see the position as hopeless. The first Cobbler to become a ward representative, who has retained this post from the inception of the panchayat system, is literate and not as poor as most members of his caste. He has spent much of his adult life in India. But he is seriously thinking of leaving the village permanently, as he sees no prospect of any real improvement in the position of the Cobblers, mainly because of lack of economic opportunities. Bali Burtel, then, in one sense, acts as the leader of the untouchables.

Bali Burtel equally needs the untouchables, primarily because of their large numbers, which give him votes at election time, since there are so few members of his own clan in the village. It was the numerical strength of the untouchables which helped to quash the motion of "no confidence" brought by the Ramas at the village assembly. He has, after all, alienated much of his traditional support from the Adikaris through the dispute about the compulsory grain savings. However, it is important to note that the Adikaris and the other high castes in the village now support the Ramas not just because they have quarrelled with Bali

Burtel, but because this support is actively solicited by the Ramas, particularly by the pandits, through powerful symbols—namely, caste and religion.

Hindus in Nepal may take women of lower (clean) castes for wives, and the children will inherit the clan of the father, but generally not his caste.[4] In this way, two persons of different caste, Brahmin and Chetri, for example, can be closely related and members of the same lineage. On the death of a member of the lineage, all the other members become polluted and should abstain from eating meat or salt. In Duari, members of a lineage keep death-pollution for each other for the maximum period of thirteen days, regardless of caste. In fact, according to a number of Sanskrit texts, this practice is not correct (Orenstein 1965). A Brahmin can only be polluted for three days by the death of a lower-caste kinsman, but a Jaisi or Chetri is polluted for thirteen days by the death of a Brahmin, and a Chetri the same by the death of a Jaisi.

When the Rama pandits returned from their studies in Kathmandu and Benares, they told the other high castes that what they were doing was incorrect and showed them the texts which supported their claim. The situation has thus been in a state of flux for some time. The pandits refuse to observe more than three days of pollution at the deaths of their lower-caste relatives. A few other Rama Brahmins have adopted the "new" ruling. This causes great annoyance, and some Jaisis and Chetris threaten to reciprocate by keeping only three days of pollution after the death of a Brahmin, although none appears to have done so as yet.

The Adikari Brahmins at first refused to accept the practices suggested by the pandits; they said that they would continue to keep the full pollution period for their Chetri relatives. However, the situation in this respect appears to have changed during 1969, the year in which Bali Burtel lost the election, and also the year in which he quarrelled with the Adikaris. At the beginning of the year, it was averred by all informants that the Adikaris kept the full pollution period, regardless of caste. But by the end of the year, one Adikari Brahmin stated that he would keep only three days for his lower-caste relatives, and an Adikari Chetri confirmed that this would probably happen in the event of a death. However, no Adikaris died during the period of my fieldwork, so it was not possible to observe what would actually happen. The fact remains, however, that what informants *said* would happen changed completely during the course of the year.

The matter has come to symbolise political alignments in the village. The pandits argue that the Adikaris, particularly the Brahmins among them, should not demean themselves by keeping long periods of pollution for lower-caste relatives and that they should also not demonstrate their ignorance of Sanskrit texts in this way. But what they are also seeking to demonstrate is their own superiority in knowledge of caste and pollution matters and the inferiority of the other villagers, particularly the other Brahmins. At the same time, the pandits are also soliciting the political support of the Adikaris. They seem to be implying that, just as the Adikaris should accept their lead in religious matters, so should they in political matters.

In this they have been partly successful. Ths Adikaris, like the Naules, see the pandits as unscrupulous and resent many of their activities; they have not forgotten how the pandits were dismissed from government service for forgery when they tried to get rid of the old Kathmandu pandit in the bhasa school or that they used equally underhanded methods in trying to remove Bali Burtel as council chairman. And yet this very unscrupulousness which makes them so personally unpopular is somehow seen to be exactly the quality which a leader ought to have. The Adikaris are often described by other villagers as "gentlemen" or by themselves as "simple and good", and they point to their legendary ancestor to whom the god Mahabe revealed himself (Legend B) precisely because the ancestor possessed these qualities. But this makes the Adikaris unsuited to be leaders. The Ramas, on the other hand, always clever, as both the villagers and they themselves point out, are the sort of people considered to make good leaders, particularly in the panchayat system.

The pandits and other Ramas also use another argument to win over the other high-castes in the village to their cause. This concerns the change in the legal status of untouchables since the revolution. The majority of high-castes have vaguely heard of the new constitution and legal code *(Mulki Ain)* of 1963, and they believe that caste has been abolished. They have also been somewhat shaken to find that many untouchables have had their debts cancelled or reduced by the land-reform office and to learn that any money lent to untouchables in the future must go through this office, thus reducing their control over their debtors. The high-castes are also well aware of the power of the untouchables' votes, since the latter form such a large proportion of the village population. Finally, and perhaps most important, they are also aware of the growing economic independence of the untouchables. It is no longer as easy for the high-castes, particularly the Brahmins, to coerce the Cobblers through economic means, as they did, for example, in the affair of Bali Burtel's school (Dispute B, Chapter 5). The high-castes assert frequently that the Cobblers are much better off than they used to be and also complain of the "high wages" which have to be paid to ploughmen and agricultural labourers. There is thus little doubt that the high-castes feel that a certain amount of change is in the wind, change which will not necessarily benefit them, and the pandits play on this. It does not mean that a revolution is feared in the village; the untouchables have no hope of achieving real power there, but it is in the interests of the high-castes to see that the untouchables do not benefit too much from the recent changes. This can best be done by a show of high-caste unity.

The Aftermath of the Election

The untouchables, in the meanwhile, are increasingly realising that as a group they have a certain amount of political power, albeit limited, because of the new resource given to them—the vote. During the election campaign, they were assiduously wooed by both candidates, and they were frequently told, "We are all equal now—caste has been abolished." Such statements had an effect on the untouchables; some of them, after all, had spent much of their adult lives in India and had witnessed the struggles there. Most migrants claim that the lot of untouchables has drastically improved in India since independence; it thus may be that they hope their lot will improve, too.

At the first village assembly to be held after the election, a petition was presented by the Cobblers to the effect that they and all the untouchables should be allowed to use the village wells. They are now only allowed to use running water from the springs, which is a serious inconvenience to many untouchables living in areas of the village where there are few springs. This proposal was greeted with consternation by the high-castes present, who obviously were not quite sure how to react, being uncertain of the law in this regard. However, Pandit Kanak Rama made an impassioned speech in which he denounced Bali Burtel's regime and attacked him for failing to develop the village, going on to say that development came through self-help and that if the untouchables needed more water, they should construct a spring or well themselves. This last point was eagerly seized upon, and it was hastily decided that a new spring, which could be used by all castes, should be constructed.

However, there seems no doubt that the Cobblers' request came as a surprise to many high-caste men, many of whom must have thought it a dangerous precedent. At the next village assembly, two charges were brought against untouchables. The first, and most relevant to the Cobblers' petition, complained that Cobblers had been eating carrion beef, of which there had been a lot available lately because of an epidemic among the cattle. Now Cobblers traditionally dispose of cattle carcases and in the process are said to eat the flesh; this practice is anathema to high-caste Hindus. Since the untouchables are outside the Hindu hierarchy, however, objection is not usually made. In this instance, what the high-caste men were doing was to remind everyone just how low and debased the Cobblers were and thereby showing the impossibility of their sharing in the use of village wells; in short, they were putting the Cobblers in their place. The Cobblers had sought to gain some slight recognition from the high-castes, to translate their new political power into ritual and status terms, and they were rebuffed.

The second matter, raised by another high-caste man, was against the Smiths of Toli, who service the whole Administrative Village and who have customers over a wider area, as well. It was claimed that these men were using an inordinate amount of wood for their work and thereby "destroying our forests". Two reasons may be advanced for this complaint. Wood is becoming increasingly scarce, and the remaining forests are officially, albeit ineffectually, protected. But almost everyone cuts down whole trees if he wants to build or chop branches and leaves for fodder and firewood. It is thus easy to accuse an enemy of technically violating the law, because he will almost certainly be guilty. (It will be remembered that the petition against Bali Burtel included an accusation about cutting down trees or allowing others to do so.) Why did the high-castes want to get the Smiths into trouble with the authorities?

The Smiths are in no doubt. They have recently become relatively prosperous, as they attract customers even from the bazaar. They maintain that the high-castes are jealous of this prosperity and dislike their having links outside the village. One Smith told me, "They want us to be dependent only upon them; they do not like us to have customers from outside or to see us getting prosperous". The Smiths are tied to the high-castes through jajmani links, and the high-castes want to keep it that way. Early in 1969, one Smith family from this village migrated to the terai permanently, taking his whole family. His fellow caste men maintained that he had been driven out by the jealous high-castes. These actions by the high-castes may have been another attempt to put in its place an untouchable group which was becoming relatively prosperous and thereby potentially independent of high-caste control.

There does seem to have been a hardening in very recent years over caste matters: this is exemplified not only by reaction to the Cobblers' request to use the wells and the difficulties encountered by the Smiths of Toli, but also by the gradual swing away from traditional death-pollution practices to the more orthodox ones advocated by the pandits. In this regard, there is an interesting contrast between two very similar cases involving villagers, which concern caste offences.

Dispute G.   *The Jaisi and the Goldsmith Girl*

In 1956, Ganga Rama, a Jaisi, later to become chairman of the village council, was a successful shopkeeper in the bazaar. A Goldsmith [untouchable] girl accused him of being the father of her child, and some of Ganga Rama's enemies in the bazaar brought a case against him for breaking caste rules (at that time such offences were punishable by law). However, Ganga Rama's brother in the police brought a counter-action against the girl for slandering his brother. Ganga Rama won the case. He was supported throughout by his brother, the Rama pandits, and other village notables. No one in the village refused to share his pipe or his water.

Dispute H.   *The Jaisi and the Cobbler Girl*

In 1969, a Duari Cobbler girl accused a Naule Jaisi of having made her pregnant. He denied it, but most villagers immediately treated him as an outcaste; even his own wives refused to cook for him, and he was forced to go live with his married sister, who sided with him. Soon, the Rama police officer, affinally linked with the Naule, and the village council chairman, Daya Rama, gave him their support; it was widely rumoured that the latter had been bribed by him. However, the rest of the villagers, including the pandits and other Brahmins, continued to insist that the Jaisi had lost his caste.

Ultimately, the Jaisi filed a suit for slander against the Cobbler girl, but the case had not been decided when I left the field; the majority of villagers were still refusing to take water from him or to smoke a pipe with him.

The circumstances of these two disputes about caste are basically very similar —a Jaisi being accused of impregnating an untouchable girl. But the villagers' reactions appear to have been quite different: Ganga Rama was not outcasted and had many supporters, including the orthodox pandits, while the Naule Jaisi was immediately treated by most villagers as if he had lost his caste. One explanation may be that Ganga Rama was a man of greater influence than the Jaisi, and so found it easier to avoid penalties.

However, I would suggest also that there is a growing emphasis on all the niceties of caste distinction in the village. To have turned a blind eye to the Jaisi's affair might have been construed as a weakening among the high-castes, who feel that their relationship with the untouchables is becoming increasingly ambiguous. After all, in the context of the law and of politics (at least, of voting), the untouchables are now equal to the high-castes; in the economic sphere, the former are increasingly independent; there is therefore a very real necessity to redefine the position of the untouchables ritually. To do so requires also a redefinition of high-caste status, thus a rejection of either lax death-pollution habits, or of the countenancing of sexual relations across the caste barrier.

This caste conflict must be seen on two levels. On the surface the untouchables now have a new political resource, the vote, and they are economically much more independent of the high-castes than in the past. But this does not mean that they have much real political or economic power, for in reality these are limited by the fact that Nepal is officially a Hindu kingdom, that most government servants are members of high castes, and that many of those in Belaspur Bazaar are linked with high-caste villagers in Duari. Untouchables are thus unlikely to be able to enforce their rights through official channels. Indeed, it can hardly be said that the untouchables, even where they are numerically as important as they are in Duari, constitute an important threat to the high-castes.

The fact remains, however, that the high-castes do feel somewhat uneasy, and this feeling has been played upon by the pandits in their struggles for power. By using the idiom of caste and religion, they have put themselves in a dominant position and have succeeded in luring the other high-castes away from Bali Burtel. At the same time, by emphasizing the independence of the untouchables they have convinced the other high-castes that a show of unity against the lower castes is to their advantage. Finally, they have found that the best method of striking at Bali Burtel is to strike at the untouchables.

NOTES

1. The Toli villagers were led by their former headman and his son, the secretary of the village council. Previously, these people had supported Bali Burtel, mainly because of a quarrel with the Ramas in the 1950s over a political party issue. However, after Bali Burtel's suspension from the chairmanship most of his powers had been temporarily handed over to the secretary. This had led to a bitter dispute between Bali Burtel and his sons, on the one hand, and the secretary and his father, on the other. Accordingly, the Toli voters gave their support to the Ramas in this election.

2. Civil servants are used as polling officers.

3. The practice of a widow's immolating herself on her husband's funeral pyre. This was very rare in Nepal and would be considered the act of an exceptionally virtuous and saintly woman.

4. To which caste the children are assigned will depend on the "mix". Children of Brahmin men and Jaisi women will be Jaisis; children of Brahmin or Jaisi men and Chetri women will be Chetris; children of Brahmin, Jaisi, or Chetri men and women of lower but still clean castes will be Chetris.

7. Conclusion

I have been examining some of the economic and political changes which have taken place in Duari village. In presenting some general conclusions about this material, I shall make some comparisons with studies of social change in other villages of both India and Nepal. During the past two decades, nearly all of these villages have been subjected to similar influences, such as economic development in the wider society and the introduction of universal adult suffrage. Since village society throughout this area is highly stratified through the idiom of caste, an important focus of interest in many studies has been the manner in which relations among different castes have been affected by these changes.

The purpose of this chapter, then, is threefold: to summarise what has gone before; to compare it with other data from South Asia; and to identify those variables which appear to be crucial to the understanding of social change at the rural level in this area, particularly of the relations between high and low— especially the untouchable—castes in the economic and political fields.

Economic Change

Many writers have maintained that no real change in social relations among castes can come about unless there is economic change first. Bailey (1957, p. 269) states, "If the ranking system is validated by differential wealth, then it will be upset by changes in the distribution of wealth." Epstein (1962, p. 334) would agree: "Thus we have established a positive correlation between economic, political, ritual and organisational change, with economic change being the determining variable."

Economic change is most likely to take place when the village is not a self-sufficient unit. In Duari, such features of the economy as migration to India began when the village land could no longer support the growing population, when untouchables, in particular, could no longer make up their deficits by working for the high-castes.[1] The rise in population affected them adversely, as they mortgaged or sold more and more of their land to the Brahmins in order to obtain cash or grain. The Brahmins, who obtained these resources from their clients, invested the surplus in loans and so became even richer. A similar process is discernible among many of the tribal peoples of Nepal: Brahmins came to their areas as immigrants and eventually succeeded in acquiring much of the land of the host communities. This happened primarily because of their access to cash, of which there has always been a shortage in the hills of Nepal, and also because of their ability to manipulate governmental machinery. There were parallel developments when high-caste Hindu settlers made contact with tribal groups in India (Fürer-Haimendorf 1967). In most parts of India, however, low—and particularly, untouchable—castes appear to have owned little or no land, in some areas being precluded from doing so by virtue of their caste.

Where people are unable to earn sufficient grain and cash to make up their deficits locally, they frequently turn to migration as a solution. For many members of tribal groups in Nepal, migration in the form of service in the Gurkhas has meant an amelioration of their economic situation (Caplan 1970, Hitchcock 1961). Untouchables in Nepal, however, have traditionally only been able to migrate to seek unskilled work in the cities of northern India, and most of their savings have been used in repaying debts and making up grain deficits, not on improving their standard of living. The same situation seems to apply to economically depressed castes in India; some of their members do go to urban centres for work, but this does not result in any long-term improvement in their position in the village (Eames 1954; Opler 1956; Cohn 1959b).

Duari's untouchables have, on the whole, been able to make ends meet by migration, and all of them do own some land, even though in most cases it is pathetically little. Untouchables who cannot maintain themselves have left some Indian villages to live permanently in the cities; this is obviously more likely to happen when they have no land to tie them to their villages. Had the Cobblers in Duari continued to lose land to the Brahmins and become totally landless, it is likely that many of them would have been forced to migrate permanently, either to India or to areas of Nepal like the terai or Lakandra Valley.[2]

The likelihood of permanent emigration from the village has diminished recently in Duari, because people can make up their deficits by working locally. Villagers of all castes have profited from the expansion of Belaspur Bazaar and the eradication of malaria in Lakandra Valley. High-caste villagers have benefited from the new jobs created in government offices and from the increased trade in the bazaar; untouchables have also found their services as labourers to be in demand. Although they have not become better off, at least their economic position is no longer deteriorating, as it seems to have been prior to the revolution.

Many studies of economic change in South Asia revealed that development has led only to a worsening of the position of the lower castes. When the local job market expands, they cannot obtain work, possibly because of caste discrimination or because they are unskilled and illiterate. Epstein (1962) reports that hardly any untouchables have found work in the sugar factories which have been established in the region of Mandya, in Mysore State; Eames (1954) notes that high-caste Thakur migrants to the big cities from the Uttar Pradesh village of Madhopur are able to obtain far better jobs than untouchable migrants; Béteille (1965) shows that it is mostly the Brahmins of Sripuram village in Tanjore who are finding clerical jobs in the cities, and not the lower, poorer castes.

In some areas, economic development has increased the demand for the services of landless untouchables as unskilled labourers, but with the end result that they are worse off than before. Instead of being employed under the traditional arrangements and rewarded in grain, as were the ploughmen in Duari, untouchables now work for daily cash wages. In India the price of grain has climbed steadily in the past few decades, and these agricultural labourers find that their wages are insufficient to buy the grain they require. Here again, Duari untouchables are peculiarly fortunate; monetisation of the labour market has not affected them adversely, since they can obtain cheap rice in Lakandra.

Nor have those untouchables in Duari who still practice their caste-specific occupations within a jajmani framework, suffered as a result of economic development. Their services are still very much in demand, since virtually no manufactured goods such as tools or clothes are imported into the bazaar (they would have to be brought from India and would be very expensive). In parts of India, however, caste specialists have often found themselves redundant, as people prefer to buy manufactured goods, which may be cheaper and of superior quality to the goods made in the village.

Only in a few instances does development appear to bring opportunities to low-caste people, and this is usually when there is a demand for services which most others are unwilling to perform because they are regarded either as degrading or polluting. The untouchables of Duari earn money by portering heavy loads of goods up from the terai or else by building houses, which involves carrying stones from the mountain quarries to the bazaar. For different reasons, the Jatavs (Camars or Cobblers) of Agra have become relatively wealthy as a result of the increased demand for the shoes they make; they have no fear of competition in this field, because leather-working is highly polluting (Lynch 1969). In the same way, the Boad Distillers and Outcastes, and the Ganjam Distillers of the Kondmals in Orissa became wealthy because of their monopoly in the liquor trade at the turn of the century; again, liquor-making is considered polluting and so would not be undertaken by other castes (Bailey 1957).

Another important factor in economic change throughout Nepal and India has been land reform, designed to help depressed peoples such as untouchables. In Duari, even though there has not been any redistribution of land, the new laws do seem to have had the effect of slowing down or halting the process whereby the untouchables mortgaged their land to the Brahmins. Fortunately, the implementation of these laws has coincided with new ways of making up cash and grain deficits by means other than borrowing, and the drying-up of credit consequent upon the new laws has not as yet created too many difficulties. In some parts of India, however, lower-castes have lost their traditional credit facilities and have found no alternative ways to make ends meet. Moreover, where they used to work land for the high-castes, they have been deprived of their tenancies, and so find their position much worse than before (Neale 1962; Luschinsky 1963; Graham 1968).

Untouchables earn money by portering heavy loads of manufactured goods up to Belaspur Bazaar from the terai, a week's journey away.

Thus it is that in most instances of expanding economies offering new opportunities, there is no real redistribution of wealth. In fact, as Epstein (1962, p. 318) points out, "Far from undermining the economic structure of any society, such economic development may even strengthen the existing pattern of economic relations." In Duari, there has not been any reallocation of resources; the Cobblers remain poor in terms of land and of the amount of cash they are able to earn, while many high-castes, besides owning much land in the village, can supplement their income by government service, and invest surplus cash in buying more land or in shopkeeping. However, what *is* important for Duari untouchables is the fact that they are now much more independent of the Brahmins in the village, since they earn an increasing part of their livelihood in Belaspur Bazaar or in Lakandra. In other words, economic relations in Duari have changed, even though the relative distribution of resources remains much the same.

Political Change in Villages

In Duari, as in most villages throughout South Asia, a new panchayat system of local government has been introduced. As one writer has said, "The newness and strangeness of the institutions cannot be underestimated" (Retzlaff 1962, p. 124). For the first time, the principle of universal suffrage has been adopted, giving the vote even to the lowliest untouchable.

Some commentators have idealised the way in which Hindu villages functioned prior to the introduction of a system of voting. Elections are seen as the cause of conflict, particularly of factionalism. This is difficult either to substantiate or to refute, since there are virtually no studies of political processes at the village level before independence in India or the revolution in Nepal. Much of this study has been concerned with the factional conflicts which have occurred since the introduction of the panchayat system into Duari village, but it is not certain whether these were old conflicts expressed in new ways or whether, as seems more likely, this type of conflict was an innovation in the village. What is clear is that, as Bujra (1970, p. 10) points out: "The seeds of factionalist dispute are always present in the existence of minor quarrels between members of the community over individual resources, actions and authority roles. Such disputes may or may not be settled by normative means, but they do not in themselves constitute factionalism. They become significant however in situations where a new field of competition over political power or resources is opened up." Thus, in Duari the quarrels between Bali Burtel and the Rama pandits began long before the establishment of the panchayat system, yet it was not until that system was introduced that factionalism along the lines of the old cleavage occurred.

In some areas of South Asia panchayats either had scarcely got off the ground by the time they were studied, or else the way in which they were constituted had made them ineffective, as in Gaon (Orenstein 1965a) or in Wangala and Dalena (Epstein 1962). But in other villages the introduction of an elective system seems to have been associated with an increase of conflict of various kinds. Why is this?

Bailey (1965, p. 17) suggests that "being linked with development, [the panchayats] dispose of important spoils. Money and contracts are routed through them, via the higher level councils. Consequently . . . disputes are no longer about trivialities. . . . [also] they are charged with definite and sometimes very complicated administrative functions."

There may, of course, be a time-lag between the establishment of the new system and the realisation of its implications by the village population. In Khalapur village, where the panchayat was at first treated with indifference by the dominant caste of Rajputs, the situation changed after the implementation of land reform had been put into the hands of the chairman and village council (Retzlaff 1962). Mayer (1963, p. 90) observed a similar reaction in Madhya Pradesh: "The number of rural leaders increased after the committee elections in 1952, and the start of the development projects, when the political and financial implications of the rural [panchayat] system became clear."

This is what happened in Duari; at first most people were not interested in the new system, and there was no competition for office. It was only after the introduction of land reform, the implementation of which was placed largely in the hands of the village council, and the abolition of the headman's office and the transfer of his tax-collecting prerogatives to the council that competition for the chairmanship became intense and led to factional conflict.

As Nicholas has pointed out, the dominant mode of political conflict in South Asian villages is vertical—that is, it is factionalism. He maintains (1966, p. 55) that "In situations of rapid social change, factions frequently arise—or become more clearly defined—because factional organization is better adapted to competition in changing situations than are the political groups that are characteristic of stable societies."

Whether, then, we view factionalism as an old, ingrained pattern in Indian villages (Lewis 1958; Retzlaff 1962; Miller 1965) or as a response to strains caused by social change (Siegal and Beals 1960), such innovations as elections have clearly discernible results. "Whereas under the traditional political structure the big men might fight out decisions affecting the entire community among themselves, now they are required to recruit support and to consciously organize factions or parties" (Nicholas 1968b, p. 271). Because factions have entered the arena of elective politics, in other words, for the first time sheer numbers have become important.

Leaders of high-caste factions may find themselves seeking the support of untouchables who now possess that most important political resource, the vote. This is particularly likely to happen where untouchables are well represented, as they are in Duari: "In the competition between upper caste political groups, with its increasing emphasis on numerical majorities . . . the sympathy and vote of the lower castes become more important. Aspiring village leaders already need to court the vote of the economically independent lower castes" (Miller 1965, p. 29). Bailey (1969, p. 30) sees this as being particularly likely when such leaders cannot be sure of getting support in traditional ways: "Would-be leaders who cannot recruit followers within the rules are tempted to bend the rules and enrol people previously disqualified." Orenstein (1959, 1963, 1965a, 1970) describes how in the village of Gaon a few of the contestants for political office sought the support of the untouchables; these leaders he terms *unsanctioned* for that very reason: "The state of transformation of caste gives them an opportunity to use oppressed groups to their advantage; and the Congress Party program gives them a justification of their support of Harijans [untouchables], support which would likely have been considered unjustifiable in the past" (1959, p. 426). This is a striking parallel with the situation in Duari, and the would-be leaders in Gaon used the same methods as did Bali Burtel, for example, "giving assistance to . . . Harijans whenever difficulties arise between the Harijans and others in the village" (1959, p. 424).

Leaders of high-caste factions, then, may also try to recruit untouchable support. However, by doing so, they may set a precedent, establish a new rule, and find that the untouchables do not merely regard themselves as part of a factional following, but begin to see themselves as a political grouping with some potential power. Bujra (1970, p. 14) makes this point clearly: "The very fact that members of other than the dominant group are brought into the political arena gives them a political significance of their own. While the faction leader may view his supporters as merely backers supporting his own bid for power, the supporters themselves may view the situation in a different light, and try to use the leader for their own ends. From being political dependents, they may become political actors in their own right." This describes the situation in Duari. Bali Burtel recruited the support of the Cobblers; he utilised his traditional ties with them and also made sure of their support by helping them when necessary (see for example, Dispute C). Cobbler support was particularly useful to him after he had lost most of his high-caste followers. However, the Cobblers themselves began to realise their political potential when "their" candidate was defeated in the 1969 election by only a few votes, and so they brought about what Bailey would term a confrontation, by demanding the use of the village wells. Had there been any educated Cobblers capable of leadership and of handling dealings between themselves and the administration, they might not have needed the services of Bali Burtel as a leader.

Various writers on South Asian politics have distinguished between factionalism (conflict on "vertical" lines) and caste ("horizontal") conflict. What are we to call the situation in Duari? There seems little doubt that at the beginning of the panchayat system, competition was between the two high-caste groupings or factions, although Bali Burtel also numbered untouchables among his supporters. The situation altered, and by the time of the election in 1969, although the leaders remained the same, the lines of cleavage were largely horizontal. It may well be that the attempt to characterize the political conflict of South Asian villages as *either* factionalism *or* caste conflict is too simplistic. As Nicholas (1968b, p. 275) has pointed out: "For the Indian peasant villages considered here, politics appear to be something of a mixture of conflict between horizontally divided social strata, and conflict between vertically divided factions." Mayer (1967, p. 124) makes much the same point: "The two kinds of alignment . . . are not necessarily mutually exclusive in a village . . . both may exist simultaneously."

Some writers have maintained that it is caste conflicts rather than factionalism which is a product of rapid social change and have attempted to suggest why it appears in some villages and not in others. Nicholas is of the opinion that this form of conflict is likely to arise after the introduction of universal suffrage in a village where the traditionally dominant caste does not have decisive numerical preponderance. Using material from a number of studies of Indian villages, he shows that "the proportions of conflict between horizontally and vertically divided groups which go together to compose the structure of politics in any community seem to be directly related to the proportions of various castes in the population" (1968b, p. 275).

However, the simple fact of numerical dominance is not sufficient for a lower caste to overthrow the traditional order and take power at an election, for when the lower castes are still economically dependent upon the higher ones, they tend to vote as they are instructed. In the Uttar Pradesh village of Khalapur, studied by Retzlaff, the dominant caste of Rajputs, who could have been defeated by an alliance of lower castes, easily won the largest number of seats on the first elected council. This was despite the efforts of some lower castes, joined by a few Brahmins and Rajputs, to break the traditional power of the Rajputs. As Retzlaff (1962, p. 60) points out: "Little had been done to alter the economic dependence of the lower castes on the rajputs, and . . . even a united bloc of lower castes would eventually have to yield". By the time of the second election, the lower castes were resigned to the situation, and, in general, each man voted for the Rajput with whom he had some such traditional tie as a farmer-retainer relationship.

In another village in Uttar Pradesh, Madhopur, studied by Cohn and others, the untouchable Camars won control of the village council.[3] The dominant caste of Thakurs, however, ignored the council and refused to carry out any of the motions it passed. Cohn (1955, p. 72) argues that economic factors were responsible for the ineffectiveness of the council: "The low castes, and particularly the Camars, lacked the economic base for a long-term fight against the Thakurs, on whom they were dependent for a livelihood." At the following election, the Thakurs took control of the council.

However, a few years later in Madhopur a number of low castes, including Camars, succeeded, against the strong opposition of the Thakurs, in building a school for their children (Rowe 1963). Their success is probably related to their greater economic independence from the Thakurs, gained mostly by migration to the cities.

The events in Madhopur bear a strong resemblance to those in Duari. Bali Burtel attempted to open a school to be attended largely by untouchables, but this was opposed by the Rama Brahmins, who put pressure on the untouchables and forced them to withdraw their children. By the time of the 1969 election, however, the untouchables had become much more independent of the Brahmins and could openly support the candidate of their choice.

External Factors

Given, then, a situation of universal suffrage, with a low caste which is numerically important and, to a large extent, independent of the higher castes, can the low caste be sure of eventual success in the struggle for power in the village? The answer depends largely on another factor, perhaps even more crucial than those already discussed. As Bujra (1970, p. 120) points out, "a subordinate group can only challenge a powerful minority when it has the advantage of external support . . . It could well be argued that in any stratified community, the direction of the lines of political division depends as much on the external political situation as it does on the internal balance of power". Nicholas (1968a, p. 296) makes the same point: "the working out of political competition in the village is seen as being powerfully influenced by a configuration of resources and rules that lies outside it in the political arenas of state and nation".

After the 1951 revolution, Nepal, like India, introduced a constitution and legal code guaranteeing equal rights for all citizens. It is widely believed in Nepal and elsewhere that caste has officially been abolished. In fact, the relevant section of the constitution (Section 10, "Right to Equality") states only that discrimination on the grounds of caste may not be made "in the application of the law" and "in respect of appointment to the government service or any other public service". Part 4 of the constitution, which also mentions untouchability and the desirability of its eradication, is preceded by the statement, "The principles laid down in this Part are for general guidance and they shall not be enforceable by any court." Even these principles are further diluted in Section 14, which states that "every person, having regard to the traditions may profess and practice his own religion as handed down from ancient times" (pp. 5, 7, 9, 10).

In Kathmandu, untouchables who tried on two occasions (once after the revolution, and once after the promulgation of the new constitution) to enter Nepal's holiest temple, Pasupatinath, were turned back by the police. At the end of 1963, the year in which the constitution was introduced, a clarification was issued by the special complaints department of the palace secretariat, stating that the caste system itself had not been abolished and that the new legal code sought merely to introduce "equality before the law". It was further stated that "those who indulge in actions prejudicial to the social customs and traditions of others will be punished" (Joshi and Rose, 1966, p. 474; see also p. 160).

Caste offences can no longer officially be tried in courts, but many, such as the dispute of the Jaisi and the Cobbler girl (Dispute H) end up in court under the guise of slander *(bejatti)*. Untouchables know that they can now send their children to school, but, aside from the economic difficulties precluding this, they claim that in the bazaar school, discrimination is practised by high-caste teachers. The land-reform laws state that land mortgaged many years ago should be returned if the creditor has received the equivalent of the original debt in the usufruct of the land, yet, unable to produce documentary evidence of ownership or to cope with the complicated mechanisms of government, very few untouchable have managed to recover lands lost in the past. When they turn for support to government agencies such as the district panchayat office or the court or the land-reform office, they are confronted by officials who are, first of all, members of high castes themselves, with little sympathy for untouchables and some of whom, furthermore, have multiplex ties with those very high-caste villagers from whom protection is needed. In some instances, untouchables find themselves dealing with clerks and messengers who are both members of high castes and fellow-villagers. Even in instances where the high castes of Duari cannot utilise their informal links directly, they are often in a better position than are untouchables to manipulate government officials and machinery, either because of their literacy and understanding of "the system" or else because of their greater wealth, which enables them to "buy" what they cannot get by other means (see Caplan 1971).

India has gone further than Nepal in its efforts to abolish untouchability and democratise its political system. The notion of egalitarianism has not only been promoted in India since independence; even during British times there were indigenous reform movements, such as the Arya Samaj and Congress, and abolition or modification of the caste system was proposed by leaders such as Gandhi and Ambedkar during the struggle for independence. After 1947 special provisions for positive discrimination in favour of Scheduled Castes and Tribes have been made in the form of reserved seats on councils, as well as reserved jobs in the civil service and places in schools and colleges. In addition, two of the major political parties in India, Congress and Communist, posit an egalitarian ideology. How are we to assess the effectiveness of these measures at the village level?

In discussing social change in India, Bailey and others[4] have distinguished two separate structures—that of the village (A) and that of the wider society (B). In this model, the two structures are seen as possessing widely differing norms and values; that of the former is based on inequality, and that of the latter on equality. Because of the premises on which these ideologies are based, "the people who work with the rules of Structure A and those who work under Structure B have difficulty in understanding what they are each doing and why they are doing it" (Bailey 1969, p. 149). However, the situation in the Kondmals of Orissa on which the model is based is atypical. This area is exceptionally isolated, and Bisipara itself an unusually self-contained village. At the time of study, the national administration was interfering little in the internal affairs of the village, and, hence, little change had taken place at that level; however, for those unable to achieve their objectives in the village, Structure B, with its courts, police, government officials, caste federations, schools, and colleges existed as an alternative. In Bisipara, the Board untouchables became wealthy, but were unable to raise their status in the village or to participate in its political affairs. As a result, Bailey reports (1957, 1964), they began to ignore village institutions and identify instead with the wider society.

But in other areas of India and in Nepal it can be shown that such a sharp cleavage between the village and the wider society does not exist. Only one structure encompassing both levels can be discerned, either because change has taken place at both levels or because there has been very little change at either level. An example of a situation where change has occurred concerns the village of Sripuram in Tanjore (Beteille 1965): there the traditionally dominant Brahmins have been displaced from political (although not economic) power by the non-Brahmins, who have both numbers and external support on their side. The external support comes from political parties and the state government, for in this area, as in much of South India, there has been a strong anti-Brahmin movement (see also Gough 1962, 1970).

At the opposite extreme, we have the situation in two villages in Uttar Pradesh, Madhopur and Khalapur. At the state level there has been little discontinuity (Nicholas 1968a), and the leadership has continued to be drawn from the political groups which traditionally have held power. As Graham (1968, p. 359) points out, "The Congress Party, both as a party of agrarian reform, and as a political organization, has relied excessively on a continuation in a modified form of traditional systems of social control, principally the control exercised within each village community by the dominant castes. . . ." In this area, in fact, there has been very little change either at village or state level. Depressed groups, such as the Camars, are able neither to enforce their rights within the village, as is evidenced by the failure of the Camar-controlled council in Madhopur, already mentioned, nor to find an alternative structure to which to turn.

Even for the relatively wealthy and sophisticated untouchables living in urban Uttar Pradesh, the Jatavs of Agra City (Lynch 1969), who sought to refer themselves to values and norms in the wider society by becoming Buddhists and founding their own political party, success has been very limited, for the wider society still treats them as untouchables.

Where there is no sharp cleavage between village and wider society, we find that villagers, particularly those who hold political power, tend to have multiplex links with persons outside the village who are in positions of power. Béteille mentions that the new leaders of Sripuram, the non-Brahmins, have many contacts with government officials, while Minturn and Hitchcock (1966) state that the court to which villagers of Khalapur take their cases is staffed by their fellow villagers of high caste! In Duari, too, as has been shown, villagers of high caste tend to have links with administrators; there is no rigid dichotomy between the village and the wider society; all share most of the same norms and values. Duari, in fact, belongs in the same category as the Uttar Pradesh villages mentioned; little real change has taken place either in the village or in the wider society of which it is a part; there has merely been accommodation to the post-revolutionary innovations. Thus, there is little likelihood that untouchables will be able substantially to improve their political position within the village. Nor is there much more hope that the wider society will offer them an alternative avenue of advancement. Indeed, because of the nature of the Nepalese political system, political betterment (that is, participation in decision-making processes at the district and national levels) can only be achieved by first gaining control of village councils. Political parties and caste federations have had a marked effect on the status of untouchables in India. In Nepal, however, such organisations are banned, and the untouchables, in effect, have nowhere to turn save to the panchayat organisation.

In this conclusion, I have attempted to follow Swartz's suggestion (1968, p. 278) to describe change in small-scale political systems by examining change in one or more of the variables present. Three important variables in the study of changing relations between the highest and lowest castes in Duari and, indeed, in most villages in South Asia, have accordingly been distinguished. First, I have examined economic development, to note, in particular, whether or not it leads to a reallocation of resources or a weakening of the ties of dependence of the lower castes upon the higher. Second, given universal adult suffrage, the demographic composition of the village, and, indeed, of the region surrounding a village, is important. Where low castes are in very small numbers, they are unlikely to be in a position to defy the higher castes, nor is their support likely to be sought by aspiring leaders. Third, the lower castes must receive some concrete support from external agencies. It is not enough merely to introduce new laws and a new constitution: these have to be enforced at the village level. Alternatively, the wider society has to provide other mechanisms which give members of lower castes some opportunity for mobility outside the village, such as government jobs, political parties, or reform movements.

NOTES

1. In the Indian Himalayan village of Sirkanda, there was no migration, apparently because it was still self-sufficient in grain (Berreman 1962).

2. An increasing influx of permanent migrants from the Far Western Hills to these areas is reported; most of them are said to be from the lowest end of the economic spectrum (McDougal 1968). Probably they are from villages where the land shortage is even greater than in Duari and where there are no new economic opportunities.

3. Cohn 1955, 1959b, 1961; Opler 1956, 1959; Opler and Singh 1948, 1952; Opler, Rowe, and Stroop 1959; Eames 1954; Luschinsky 1963.

4. Bailey 1969; Swartz, Turner, and Tuden 1966; Swartz 1968.

Bibliography

Bailey, F. G. 1957. *Caste and the Economic Frontier.* Manchester University Press.

———. 1964. "Two villages in Orissa." In *Closed Systems and Open Minds,* ed. M. Gluckman. Edinburgh: Oliver and Boyd.

———. 1965. "Decisions by Consensus in Councils and Committees: with Special Reference to Village and Local Government in India." In *Political Systems and the Distribution of Power,* ed. M. Banton. London: Tavistock.

———. 1968. "Parapolitical Systems." In *Local-Level Politics,* ed. M. J. Swartz. Chicago: Aldine.

———. 1969. *Stratagems and Spoils.* Oxford: Blackwell.

Beals, A. R. 1955. "Inter-play Among Factors of Change in a Mysore Village." In *Village India,* ed. M. Marriott. Chicago: University of Chicago Press.

Berreman, G. D. 1960. "Cultural Variability in the Himalayan Hills." *American Anthropologist* 62.

———. 1962. "Caste and Economy in the Himalayas." *Economic Development and Cultural Change* 10.

———. 1963. *Hindus of the Himalayas.* Berkeley and Los Angeles: University of California Press.

———. 1964. "Brahmins and Shamans in Pahari Religion." *Journal of Asian Studies* 23.

———. 1970. "Pahari Culture: Diversity and Change in the Lower Himalayas." In *Change and Continuity in India's Villages,* ed. K. Ishwaran. New York: Columbia University Press.

Béteille, A. 1965. *Caste, Class and Power.* Berkeley and Los Angeles: University of California Press.

Bujra, J. M. 1970. "Factions and Factionalism." Unpublished manuscript.

Caplan, L. 1967. "Some Political Consequences of State Land Policy in East Nepal." *Man* (N.S.) 2.

———. 1970. *Land and Social Change in East Nepal.* Berkeley and Los Angeles: University of California Press.

———. 1971. "Cash and Kind: Two Media of "Bribery" in Nepal." *Man* (N.S.) 6.

Cohn, B.S. 1955. "The Changing Status of a Depressed Caste." In *Village India,* ed. M. Marriott. Chicago: University of Chicago Press.

———. 1959a. "Some Notes on Law and Change in North India." *Economic Development and Cultural Change* 8.

———. 1959b. "Madhopur Revisited," *Economic Weekly* 2.

———. 1961. "The Pasts of an Indian Village." *Comparative Studies in Society and History* 3.

Cool, J. C. 1967. *The Far Western Hills: Some Longer Term Considerations.* Report to His Majesty's Government, Kathmandu. Mimeographed.

Eames, E. 1954. "Some Aspects of Urban Migration from a Village in North Central India." *Eastern Anthropologist* 8.

Epstein, T. S. 1962. *Economic Development and Social Change in South India.* Manchester University Press.

Firth, R. 1957. "Introduction to Factions in Indian and Overseas Indian Societies." *British Journal of Sociology* 8.

Fürer-Haimendorf, C. von 1956. "Elements of Newar Social Structure." *Journal of the Royal Anthropological Institute* 82.

_____. 1957. "The Inter-relations of Castes and Ethnic Groups in Nepal." *Bulletin of the* [London] *School of Oriental and African Studies* 20.

_____. 1959. "Status Differences in a High Hindu Caste of Nepal." *Eastern Anthropologist* 12.

_____. 1960. "Caste in the Multi-ethnic Society of Nepal." *Contributions to Indian Sociology* 4.

_____. 1963. "Caste and Politics in South Asia." In *Politics and Society in India,* ed. C.H. Phillips. London: Allen and Unwin.

_____. 1966. "Unity and Diversity in the Chetri Caste of Nepal." In *Caste and Kin in Nepal, India and Ceylon,* ed. C. von Fürer-Haimendorf. Bombay: Asia Publishing House.

_____. 1967. "The Position of the Tribal Populations in Modern India." In *India and Ceylon: Unity and Diversity,* ed. P. Mason. London: Oxford University Press.

Gough, K. 1962. "Caste in a Tanjore Village." In *Aspects of Caste in South India, Ceylon and North-west Pakistan,* ed. E.R. Leach. Cambridge: Cambridge University Press.

_____. 1970. "Palakhara: Social and Religious Change in Central Kerala." In *Change and Continuity in India's Villages,* ed. K. Ishwaran. New York: Columbia University Press.

Graham, B. D. 1968. "The Succession of Factional Systems in the Uttar Pradesh Congress Party, 1937–1966." In *Local-Level Politics,* ed. M.J. Swartz. Chicago: Aldine.

Hamilton, F. 1819. *An Account of the Kingdom of Nepal, and of the Territories Annexed to this Dominion by the House of Gorkha.* Edinburgh: Constable.

Hitchcock, J. 1961. "A Nepalese Hill Village and Indian Employment." *Asian Survey* 1.

_____. 1963. "Some Effects of Recent Change in Rural Nepal." *Human Organization* 22.

_____. 1966. *The Magars of Banyan Hill.* New York: Holt, Rinehart & Winston.

Joshi, B. L., and Rose, L. E. 1966. *Democratic Innovations in Nepal.* Berkeley and Los Angeles: University of California Press.

Kolenda, P. M. *See Mahar, P.M.*

Lewis, O. 1954. *Group Dynamics in a North Indian Village: a Study of Factions.* New Delhi: Programme Evaluation Organization Planning Commission, Government of India.

_____. 1958. *Village Life in Northern Indian.* Urbana: University of Illinois Press.

Luschinsky, M. S. 1963. "Problems of Culture Change in the Indian Village." *Human Organization* 22.

Lynch, O. 1969. *The Politics of Untouchability.* New York: Columbia University Press.

McDougal, C. 1968. *Village and Household Economy in Far Western Nepal.* Kirtipur, Nepal: Tribhuvan University.

Mahar, P. M. 1960. "Changing Religious Practices of an Untouchable Caste." *Economic Development and Cultural Change* 8.

_____. 1968. "Region, Caste and Family Structure: A Comparative Study of the Indian 'Joint' Family." In *Structure and Change in Indian Society*, eds. M. Singer and B. S. Cohn. Chicago: Aldine.

Mayer, A. C. 1963. "Some Political Implications of Community Development in India." *European Journal of Sociology* 4.

_____. 1967. "Caste and Local Politics in India." In *India and Ceylon: Unity and Diversity*, ed. P. Mason. London: Oxford University Press.

Miller, D. F. 1965. "Factions in Indian Village Politics." *Pacific Affairs* Spring.

Minturn, L., and Hitchcock, J. 1966. *The Rajputs of Khalapur*. New York: Wiley.

Neale, W.C. 1962. *Economic Change in Rural India: Land Tenure in Uttar Pradesh, 1800–1955*. New Haven: Yale University Press.

Nepal Government. 1962. *Sample Census of Agriculture*. Kathmandu.

_____. 1963. *The Constitution of Nepal* (English Translation). Kathmandu.

Nicholas, R. W. 1965. "Factions: a Comparative Analysis." In *Political Systems and the Distribution of Power*, ed. M. Banton. London: Tavistock.

_____. 1966. "Segmentary Factional Political Systems." In *Political Anthropology*, eds. M. J. Swartz, V. W. Turner, and A. Tuden. Chicago: Aldine.

_____. 1968*a*. "Rules, Resources and Political Activity." In *Local-Level Politics*, ed. M. J. Swartz. Chicago: Aldine.

_____. 1968*b*. "Structures of Politics in the Villages of Southern Asia." In *Structure and Change in Indian Society*, eds. M. Singer and B. S. Cohn. Chicago: Aldine.

Okada, F. E. 1957. "Ritual Brotherhood: A Cohesive Factor in Nepalese Society." *Southwestern Journal of Anthropology* 13.

Opler, M. 1956. "The Extensions of an Indian Village." *Journal of Asian Studies* 16.

_____. 1959. "Factors of Tradition and Change in a Local Election in Rural India." In *Leadership and Political Institutions in India*, eds. R. L. Park and I. Tinker. Princeton: Princeton University Press.

Opler, M., and Singh, R. 1948. "The Division of Labor in an Indian Village." In *A Reader in General Anthropology*, ed. C. Coon. New York: Henry Holt and Co.

_____. 1952. "Economic, Political and Social Change in a Village of North Central India." *Human Organization* 11.

Opler, M., Rowe, W. L., and Stroop, M. L. 1959. "Indian National Elections in a Village Context." *Human Organization* 18.

Orenstein, H. 1959. "Leadership and Caste in a Bombay Village." In *Leadership and Political Institutions in India*, eds. R. L. Park and I. Tinker. Princeton: Princeton University Press.

_____. 1963. "Village, Caste and the Welfare State." *Human Organization* 22.

_____. 1965*a*. *Gaon: Conflict and Cohesion in an Indian Village*. Princeton: Princeton University Press.

_____. 1965*b*. "The Structure of Hindu Caste Values: A Preliminary Study of Hierarchy and Ritual Defilement." *Ethnology* 4.

_____. 1970. "Gaon: The Changing Political System of a Maharashtrian Village." In *Change and Continuity in India's Villages*, ed. K. Ishwaran. New York: Columbia University Press.

Regmi, M. C. 1963. *Land Tenure and Taxation in Nepal.* 4 vols. *The State as Landlord: Raikar Tenure.* Vol. 1. Berkeley: University of California Institute of International Studies.

Retzlaff, R. 1962. *Village Government in India.* Bombay: Asia Publishing House.

Ripley, D. 1953. *Search for the Spiny Babbler: Bird-Hunting in Nepal.* London: Victor Gollancz.

Rosser, C. 1966. "Social Mobility in the Newar Caste System." In Fürer-Haimendorf, 1966.

Rowe, W. L. 1963. "Changing Rural Class Structure and the Jajmani System." *Human Organization* 22.

Siegal, B. J., and Beals, A. R. 1960. "Pervasive Factionalism." *American Anthropologist* 62.

Swartz, M. J. 1968. "Rules, Resources and Groups in Political Contests." In *Local-Level Politics,* ed. M. J. Swartz. Chicago: Aldine.

―――, Turner, V. W., and Tuden, A. 1966. *Political Anthropology.* Chicago: Aldine.

Tucci, G. 1962. *Nepal: The Discovery of the Malla.* London: Allen and Unwin.

Worth, R. M., and Shah, N. K. 1969. *Report of the National Health Survey, 1965–1966.* Honolulu: University of Hawaii Press.

INDEX